THE FICTION OF JACK LONDON

A Chronological Bibliography

Jack London as a young man is portrayed by artist Peter Van Valkenburgh in a 1941 sketch.
(*By permission of The Director, The Bancroft Library.*)

The Fiction
of
Jack London

A Chronological Bibliography

Compiled and Annotated by
DALE L. WALKER
The University of Texas at El Paso

with Research and Editing by
JAMES E. SISSON III
Berkeley, California

TEXAS WESTERN PRESS
THE UNIVERSITY OF TEXAS AT EL PASO
1972

Library of Congress Catalog Card No. 70-190575

ISBN 87404-044-2

This work is gratefully dedicated
to the late

JOAN LONDON

[1901-1971]

the pre-eminent biographer of Jack London
and friend to all interested in her father
and his work.

Joan London with Dale L. Walker in a photograph taken November 22, 1966 following a commemorative meeting at the University of Washington in Seattle; Joan London was the principal speaker. The date marked the fiftieth anniversary of Jack London's death. (Photo by George H. Tweney.)

INTRODUCTION

৵§ THIS WORK has its most immediate origin in the biblio-graphic article on Jack London which I contributed to the first issue of *American Literary Realism, 1875-1910* (Fall 1967), a journal published by the Department of English, The University of Texas at Arlington. In developing the portion of the article having to do with needed areas of London scholarship, I con-tacted several of the most prominent London scholars; among them: Dr. Hensley Woodbridge of Southern Illinois University, London bibliographer and editor of the *Jack London Newsletter;* Dr. Franklin Walker of Mills College, Oakland, California, au-thor of *Jack London and the Klondike, San Francisco's Literary Frontier, The Seacoast of Bohemia,* and many other works; and Mrs. Joan London Miller, daughter of the author and his bio-grapher *(Jack London and His Times).* All expressed the belief that no definitive or scholarly London biography had yet been written and precious little sound critical work despite the fact that the opportunity for both has existed for more than a half century. Exceptions to the latter case, that of sound criticism, cited by these experts included work by Maxwell Geismar, Philip Foner, Charles Walcutt, Arthur Calder-Marshall, Earle Labor, Alfred Shivers, Clell Peterson, King Hendricks, and Vil M. Bykov.

In 1966 I had the privilege of meeting and interviewing Joan London in Seattle, Washington, and thereafter enjoyed four years of illuminating correspondence with her, ending with a final letter just two months before her death in January, 1971. In a letter to me dated January 26, 1967, Joan London wrote: "Which biography do I think comes closest to being definitive? None of them remotely approach it. Mine certainly had no such pretension. More serious critical study needs to be done too and it will not be done by those who know Jack London only from *The Call of the Wild* and *The Sea Wolf.*"

Franklin Walker echoed these sentiments, writing me ". . . too much has been done to popularize London's life — the illegitimacy, drinking, marriages, suicide, etc. More is needed to present him adequately as a craftsman. . . ."

Hensley Woodbridge has also observed: "It seems to me that too much has been written based on too little knowledge of London's work. Only a thorough knowledge of London's fiction would prepare one to write on any part of it."

These observations, identical to my own thoughts in nearly twenty years of interest in Jack London, represent the origin of the present work, and the source of what I hope will be its usefulness as a guide for those who wish to know something more than the ordinary about Jack London himself as well as about his work. In the neglected fiction, I believe, there are neglected ideas worth attention.

Jack London's fictional canon alone is a prodigious one for a man who began writing professionally in 1899 and who died in 1916. Of the fifty-three books that bear his name, forty-one are works of fiction. These include twenty-two novels and nineteen short story collections.* The latter include all but twenty-eight of the 188 presently-known short stories by Jack London that have been published.

Add to this output London's published essays, articles, poems, plays, reviews, separately published letters, and newspaper work (a total of something over 400 items which are deserving of their own, separate, bibliography), and one has a view of this remarkable literary productivity.

In examining all of the London stories and novels in their original published form, it became clear that many errors had occurred in previous bibliographies — errors in titles of stories, periodical titles, in "classifying" non-fiction work as fiction, in the dates of appearances of certain works, and errors of omission.

*Throughout this work, *John Barleycorn* and *Hearts of Three* are considered novels although the former is sometimes viewed as autobiography, the latter as a "movie scenario." In addition, for the purposes of this work, *Smoke Bellew* is considered a "collection," and *The Kempton-Wace Letters* is not included as a work of fiction.

These errors have been rectified herein; and, for example, the present work: lists for the first time the newly-discovered Bret Harte-type London story "A Northland Miracle," (entry 188); notes for the first time that "The Whale Tooth" (entry 103) was published in England, under a different title, three years before its American appearance; is the first to recognize that "The Captain of the Susan Drew" (entry 172) and "Poppy Cargo" are one and the same story; explains for the first time the complicated matter of the publication of "An Old Soldier's Story" (entry 13) and "Old Baldy" (entry 19); lists the true first appearance of "The Unmasking of the Cad" (entry 162); and is the first to offer any explanation of the confused dating of London's stories that appeared in the periodical *Lady's Realm*.

In addition, the present work has several other attributes: it is the first London bibliography to concentrate solely on the author's fiction — his most important and lasting work; it is the first full-length *annotated* London bibliography; it is the first to list unpublished plays and their productions that were drawn from certain of the author's fictional works, and to cite the fees the author received for certain of his works, thereby giving a fuller view of his extraordinary popularity in the first years of the twentieth century; and, because of its annotated format, this work is the first to attempt to cite important critical sources of discussion on key fictional works by the author, to make certain pertinent observations on these works (as, for example, the genesis of the memorable opening lines of London's most renowned short story, "To Build a Fire"), and to suggest that certain fictional works ought to be compared to others — frequently others by London himself — for a better understanding of them.

London sold his fiction production — 188 short stories and the sixteen novels that were serialized before their hard-cover publication — to an astonishing total of sixty-eight different periodicals. Of these, only three published more than eight of his fiction pieces: *Cosmopolitan Magazine* (leading the list with twenty-nine of London's fiction works published), *The Saturday Evening Post* (with eighteen), and *The Youth's Companion* (with seventeen.)

This fiction output, divided among short stories, novels, and collections of stories (some of which contain stories written expressly for the collection), was distributed as the chart below indicates, including the two non-professional years before 1899:

Year	Stories	Novels	Collections
1895	6		
1897	1		
1899	16		
1900	15		1
1901	11		1
1902	16	2	1
1903	9	1	
1904	2	1	1
1905	10	1	1
1906	9	1	1
1907	8.	1	1
1908	10	1	
1909	13	1	
1910	12	1	1
1911	24	1	2
1912	10		3
1913	1	3	1
1914	1	1	1
1915		2	
1916	1	1	1
[London's death: 22 November 1916]			
1917	2	2	
1918	6	1	1
1919	2		1
1922	1		1
1924	1		
1926	1		
1963		1	

The table shows that in his last years, London turned away from the short story toward the novel — seven novels in the last four years of his life as against only three short stories.† It shows too that in the more tranquil year of 1911, following the *Snark* voyage and the beginning of his building of "Wolf House" and

†Three of the novels and at least eleven of the stories published posthumously were also written during this period.

the "Beauty Ranch," London reached his peak of productivity — twenty-four stories, one novel, and two collections of stories published in that single, stunning year.

Aside from the twenty-eight uncollected stories, which are difficult but not impossible to obtain (this work lists extra sources for those reprinted since their original publication), the canon is actually a rather easy and enjoyably assailable body of work. For anyone attempting to write meaningfully, either critically or biographically — or any combination of the two — about this extraordinary man and his always fascinating, sometimes brilliant, works of fiction, it is worth the effort to read all of them.

One final comment on the usefulness of the present work: some eighty *different* reference sources are listed within the 140-odd annotations accompanying the 229 entries. It is believed that these eighty sources represent some of the most significant of all the published biographical and critical works on Jack London to the present day.

Although this is a bibliography of Jack London's fictional work, all fifty-three of the author's books have been listed separately, by title, publisher, and, when known, date of publication, at the end of the fiction listings. It might be pointed out that all but four of London's books have appeared in foreign editions, most of them in several languages, a few in as many as fifty-eight languages including Esperanto. Some 400 anthologies and collections may be found in thirty-six of these languages, often in many-volumed sets. An excellent view of Jack London's works in foreign translation may be found in *Jack London: A Bibliography*, compiled by Hensley Woodbridge, John London, and George H. Tweney (Georgetown, Calif.: The Talisman Press, 1966).

—DALE L. WALKER

El Paso, Texas: October, 1971

KEY TO COLLECTIONS

At the end of each entry will be seen a code abbreviation to help the reader locate each story in one of Jack London's nineteen short story collections, or in the rare instance in which a short story was included in a non-fiction collection such as *Revolution & Other Essays* and *The Human Drift*. Entries marked "Unc." are to be found only in their original periodical appearance unless otherwise indicated in the note accompanying the entry.

[CF]	*Children of the Frost*
[DC]	*Dutch Courage & Other Stories*
[FM]	*The Faith of Men & Other Stories*
[GHF]	*The God of His Fathers & Other Stories*
[HD]	*The Human Drift*
[HP]	*The House of Pride & Other Tales of Hawaii*
[LF]	*Lost Face*
[LL]	*Love of Life & Other Stories*
[MF]	*Moon-Face & Other Stories*
[NB]	*The Night-Born*
[OMM]	*On the Makaloa Mat*
[R]	*Revolution & Other Essays*
[RO]	*The Red One*
[SB]	*Smoke Bellew*
[SOW]	*The Son of the Wolf*
[SS]	*A Son of the Sun*
[SST]	*South Sea Tales*
[STST]	*The Strength of the Strong*
[TFP]	*Tales of the Fish Patrol*
[TT]	*The Turtles of Tasman*
[Unc.]	Uncollected Story
[WGL]	*When God Laughs & Other Stories*

THE FICTION OF JACK LONDON

A Chronological Bibliography

1895

1. " 'Frisco Kid's' Story" — *The* (Oakland, Calif.) *High School Aegis*, v. 10 (February 15, 1895), 2-3. [Unc.]

   A short dialect tale of "the road." Reprinted in: *The High School Aegis*, v. 18 (May 9, 1899), 6-7; the *Class Aegis June* 1901, pp. [45]-[47]; *San Francisco Examiner*, December 3, 1916, p. 2E; *The Daily Californian Weekly Magazine* (Berkeley), November 12, 1968, pp. 9, 11-12.

2. "Sakaicho, Hona Asi and Hakadaki" — *The* (Oakland) *High School Aegis*, v. 10 (April 19, 1895), 4-5. [Unc.]

   Reprinted in *The Daily Californian Weekly Magazine*, November 12, 1968, pp. 9, 13.

3. "A Night's Swim in Yeddo Bay" — *The* (Oakland) *High School Aegis*, v. 10 (May 27, 1895), 10-12. [Unc.]

   This is the first version of the story "In Yeddo Bay," (entry 66), later drawn in greater detail and included in the posthumous collection DC.

4. "Who Believes in Ghosts!" — *The* (Oakland) *High School Aegis*, v. 10 (October 21, 1895), 1-4. [Unc.]

   Reprinted in *The Daily Californian Weekly Magazine*, November 12, 1968, pp. 8, 13.

5. "And 'Frisco Kid Came Back" — *The* (Oakland) *High School Aegis*, v. 10 (November 4, 1895), 2-4. [Unc.]

   Reprinted in the *The Oakland Herald*, April 17, 1907, p. 16.

6. " 'One More Unfortunate' " — *The* (Oakland) *High School Aegis*, v. 10 (December 18, 1895), 12-14. [Unc.]

   This tale was undoubtedly inspired by London's reading of Thomas Hood's "The Bridge of Sighs," a poem about a similar suicide, the first line of which is "One more unfortunate." Probably also influenced by the author's reading of Ouida's *Signa* (1875).

1897

7. "Two Gold Bricks" — *The Owl* (Boston, New York), v. 3 (September 1897), 43-48. [Unc.]

   For another printing of this little dialect tale, see Wm. McDevitt's monograph *Jack London's First* (San Francisco: Recorder-Sunset Press, 1946), pp. 12-17.

1899

8. "To the Man on the Trail" — *Overland Monthly*, v. 33 (January 1899),
    36-40. [sow]

Writing to his friend Cloudesley Johns on February 27, 1899, London said: "The
compositors made some bad mistakes, the worst being a willful change in the
title, and a most jarring one. It was plainly typewritten 'To the Man on Trail';
this they printed 'To the Man on the Trail.' What trail? The thing was abstract."
Quoted in Charmian K. London, *The Book of Jack London* (New York: The
Century Co., 1921), I, 280. Hereafter cited as *Book of Jack London*. Commonly,
this tale is listed as the story marking London's debut as a professional writer.
Although the story is a fine one, its publication did not prove an auspicious beginning. The moribund *Overland* not only failed to send London a courtesy copy
of the issue it appeared in, but — more important to the impecunious young
writer — it failed to send the promised $5 purchase fee for it. London finally had
to storm the *Overland* offices to extract the $5 from the pockets of Roscoe Eames
and Edward Biron Payne of the magazine's staff. For one version of this dreary
episode in the *Overland's* history, see Irving Stone, *Sailor on Horseback: The
Biography of Jack London* (Boston: Houghton Mifflin Co., 1938), pp. 113-116,
cited hereafter as *Sailor on Horseback*. Significantly, this famous book was sub-
titled "A Biographical Novel" in all editions after the first. For a different version
of the same episode, see James Howard Bridge, *Millionaires and Grub Street*
(New York: Brentano's, 1931), pp. 200, 202. Bridge was *Overland* editor at the
time of the encounter.

9. "The White Silence" — *Overland Monthly*, v. 33 (February 1899),
    138-142. [sow]

The *Overland* paid London $7.50 for this tale which Irving Stone calls "one of
our imperishable classics of the frozen country." (*Sailor on Horseback*, p. 114.)

10. "The Son of the Wolf" — *Overland Monthly*, v. 33 (April 1899), 335-
    343. [sow]

11. "The Men of Forty-Mile" — *Overland Monthly*, v. 33 (May 1899),
    [388], 401-405. [sow]

12. "A Thousand Deaths" — *The Black Cat* (Boston), [v. 4] (May 1899),
    33-42. [Unc.]

London later said he was "literally and literarily" saved by the $40 H. D.
Umbstaetter paid him for this story. See London's introduction to Umbstaetter's
The Red Hot Dollar & Other Stories From the Black Cat (Boston: L. C. Page
& Co., 1911), pp. v-ix. London also wrote in his manuscript record that the $40
was "first money received for a story from a magazine." (King Hendricks and
Irving Shepard, eds., *Letters from Jack London*. New York: The Odyssey Press,
1965, p. 39.) Hereafter cited as *Letters*.
For a reprinting of this rare story, see *The Magazine of Fantasy and Science
Fiction*, 33 (September 1967), pp. 91-99; and *The London Collector* (Cedar
Springs, Mich., Richard Weiderman, editor), No. 2 (April 1971), pp. 3-13.

13. "An Old Soldier's Story" — *Orange Judd Farmer*, v. 23 (May 20, 1899), 659; *American Agriculturist*, v. 63 (May 20, 1899), 659; *The New England Homestead*, v. 38 (May 20, 1899), 659. [Unc.]

"The *American Agriculturist*, of New York, was made a weekly journal in 1894 and became the central edition of a system of regional magazines that included *The New England Homestead* of Springfield, Mass., and the *Orange Judd Farmer* of Chicago." (Frank Luther Mott, *A History of American Magazines* — 1885-1905. Cambridge, Mass.: Harvard University Press, 1957, p. 337.)

Charmian K. London erroneously listed this story as having appeared in *Evenings at Home* in May, 1894. (See bibliography in her *Book of Jack London*, II, 397). "Evenings at Home" was a section of *Orange Judd Farmer, American Agriculturist*, and *The New England Homestead*. Charmian London also gives the story's title as "On Furlough," but the present survey has found no version under that title.

14. "In a Far Country" — *Overland Monthly*, v. 33 (June 1899), 540-549. [sow]

Franklin Walker says this tale "clearly owes a good deal to Conrad's story" ("An Outpost of Progress" which had appeared the year before in the volume *Tales of Unrest*). See Walker's *Jack London and the Klondike: The Genesis of an American Writer* (San Marino, Calif.: The Huntington Library, 1966), p. 239, hereafter cited as *Jack London and the Klondike*. W. Somerset Maugham also wrote of a similar situation in the story "The Outstation."

15. "The Priestly Prerogative" — *Overland Monthly*, v. 34 (July 1899), 59-65. [sow]

16. "The Handsome Cabin Boy" — *The Owl Magazine*, v. 7 (July 1899), 45-50. [Unc.]

London received $1.50 for this "skit" as he called it. "But it more than paid for the stamps I had wasted on the thing . . .," he said (*Letters*, p. 50.) In the story "In a Far Country," (entry 14), he had mentioned "The Handsome Cabin Boy" as one of the Klondikers' songs.

17. "The Wife of a King" — *Overland Monthly*, v. 34 (August 1899), 112-119. [sow]

See entry 44.

18. "In the Time of Prince Charley" — *Conkey's Home Journal* (Chicago), v. 5 (September 1899), 1-3. [Unc.]

A distinct departure for London — then turning out reams of Klondike fiction — was this tale having to do with the days of George II; the locale, Scotland.

19. "Old Baldy" — *Orange Judd Farmer*, v. 127 (September 16, 1899), 281-282; *American Agriculturist*, v. 64 (September 16, 1899), 281-

282; *The New England Homestead*, v. 39 (September 16, 1899), 281-282. [Unc.]

See note on entry 13. Mott's explanation of the relationship between these periodicals explains why some of London's stories appeared in different magazines at the same time in this period. He has been accused of selling his old stories, using new titles, "'. . . to obscure journals which were unlikely to meet the eyes of the first purchasers.'" (Nancy Barr Mavity, "Jack London Rare Works Discovered," *Oakland Tribune*, November 28, 1932, p. B3.) But at least in some instances the various publications of the same tale were clearly not of London's design.

20. "The Rejuvenation of Major Rathbone" — *Conkey's Home Journal*, v. 6 (November 1899), 5-6, 29. [Unc.]

21. "The King of Mazy May" — *The Youth's Companion*, v. 73 (November 30, 1899), 629-630. [Unc.]

22. "The Wisdom of the Trail" — *Overland Monthly*, v. 34 (December 1899), 541-544. [SOW]

23. "A Daughter of the Aurora" — *[San Francisco Wave] The Christmas Wave*, 1899, pp. 9-10, 16. [GHF]

1900

24. "An Odyssey of the North" — *The Atlantic Monthly*, v. 85 (January 1900), 85-100. [SOW]

The Atlantic asked London to cut 3,000 words from the opening section of this story and paid him $120 for publication rights. The original version of the story ran 12,250 words and London later wrote to Cloudesley Johns (August 10, 1899), ". . . I only succeeded in getting it down to an even ten thousand." (*Letters*, p. 50.) London's first book contract, for the volume of short stories *The Son of the Wolf*, was signed on December 21, 1899.

25. "A Lesson in Heraldry" — *The National Magazine* (Boston), v. 11 (March 1900), 635-640. [Unc.]

---

1. *The Son of the Wolf* — Boston: Houghton, Mifflin Co., April 7, 1900. [SOW]

---

26. "The End of the Chapter" — *San Francisco News Letter and California Advertiser*, v. 23 (June 9, 1900), 22-23. [Unc.]

27. "Uri Bram's God" — San Francisco *Examiner, Sunday Examiner Magazine,* June 24, 1900, p. 10. [GHF]

Also known as "Which Make Men Remember," in GHF, and "The Dead Horse Trail" in *Ellery Queen's Mystery Magazine,* 43 (June 1964), pp. 60-66. London's description of the terrible Dead Horse Trail — ". . . The horses died like mosquitos in the first frost, and from Skaguay to Bennett they rotted in heaps. They died at the Rocks, they were poisoned at the Summit, and they starved at the Lakes; they fell off the trail, what there was of it, or they went through it; in the river they drowned under their loads, or were smashed to pieces against the boulders. . . ." — is an authentic piece of Klondike history, quoted extensively by Pierre Berton, historian of the Klondike gold rush of '98. See his *Klondike Fever* (New York: Alfred A. Knopf, 1958), pp. 152-157. (See also entry 105.)

28. "Even Unto Death" — *The* (San Francisco) *Evening Post Magazine,* July 28, 1900, pp. 4-5. [Unc.]

This story is an early version of "Flush of Gold," see entry 107.

29. "Grit of Women" — *McClure's Magazine,* v. 15 (August 1900), 324-330. [GHF]

This story should be compared with "Wonder of Woman" (entry 170). *McClure's* accepted the story on condition that London would revise the opening and "eliminate the profanity." He told them to go ahead and make the changes themselves. (*Letters,* p. 92.) But he was not always so cooperative in such matters.

30. "Jan, the Unrepentant" — *Outing* (Albany, N. Y.), v. 36 (August 1900), 474-477. [GHF]

31. "Their Alcove" — *The Woman's Home Companion,* v. 27 (September 1900), 13. [Unc.]

32. "The Man With the Gash" — *McClure's Magazine,* v. 15 (September 1900), 459-465. [GHF]

This story was lost for a time at *Collier's Weekly,* then returned and refused by several other magazines before *McClure's* accepted it. (*Book of Jack London,* I, 331.)

33. "The Proper 'Girlie' " — *The Smart Set,* v. 2 (October-November 1900), 117-119. [Unc.]

34. "Thanksgiving on Slav Creek" — *Harper's Bazar,* v. 33 (November 24, 1900), 1879-1884. [Unc.]

Compare with "The Stampede to Squaw Creek" (entry 150). *Harper's Bazar* became *Bazaar* after 1929.

35. "Dutch Courage" — *The Youth's Companion*, v. 74 (November 29, 1900), 622-623. [DC]

36. "Where the Trail Forks" — *Outing*, v. 37 (December 1900), 276-282. [GHF]

   It is instructive to compare the ending of this story to that of *The Call of the Wild*, entry **6**.

37. "The Great Interrogation" — *Ainslee's Magazine* (New York), v. 6 (December 1900), 394-402. [GHF]

   Ainslee's cut 500 words from this story without asking London's permission. He received $125 for it. (*Letters*, pp. 117-118.) The story was the basis for a one-act play of the same name by London and Lee Bascom (Mrs. George Hamilton Marsden). It was produced throughout the United States from 1905 to 1911.

38. "Semper Idem" — *The Black Cat*, v. 6 (December 1900), 24-28. [WGL]

   London wrote to Cloudesley Johns on July 23, 1900, "Did you read that storiette of mine, 'Semper Idem; Semper Fidelis'? . . . Well I have sent it everywhere. At last I sent it to *Black Cat*. I would have sold it for a dollar." (*Book of Jack London*, I, 344.) He received $50 for it.

1901

39. "A Relic of the Pliocene" — *Collier's Weekly*, v. 26 (January 12, 1901), 17, 20. [FM]

   This story was reprinted as "The Angry Mammoth" in *The Magazine of Fantasy and Science Fiction*, 16 (May 1959), pp. 99-107.

40. "Siwash" — *Ainslee's Magazine*, v. 7 (March 1901), 108-115. [GHF]

41. "The Law of Life" — *McClure's Magazine*, v. 16 (March 1901), 435-438. [CF]

   McClure's bought this story, "Grit of Women," and the essay "The Question of the Maximum," paying $300 for the two stories, an unspecified sum for the essay. (*Letters*, pp. 91, 106.)

42. "The Lost Poacher" — *The Youth's Companion*, v. 75 (March 14,1901), 121-122. [DC]

43. "At the Rainbow's End" — *The Pittsburg* (Pa.) *Leader*, March 24, 1901, p. 31. [GHF]

44. "The Scorn of Woman" — *Overland Monthly*, v. 37 (May 1901), 978-991. [GHF]

   Freda Moloof, a Dawson City figure who billed herself as "the Turkish Whirlwind Danseuse," was used as the pattern for Freda in this story. She also appears in "The Wife of a King" (entry 17), and there is a "Freda" in *Burning Daylight*, entry **18**. Years after the Klondike days, London ran into Freda Moloof doing her muscle dance at an Oakland street fair. He later sent her a copy of GHF in which "The Scorn of Women" appeared. (In its original appearance it was "Woman.") See Richard O'Connor, *Jack London, A Biography*. Boston: Little, Brown & Co., 1964, pp. 97-98 fn. London's play of the same title (1906) was based on this story.

45. "The Minions of Midas" — *Pearson's Magazine* (New York), v. 11 (May 1901), 698-705. [MF]

In a letter to Johns, dated March 24, 1901, London indicates that this tale was originally directed to *The Black Cat*. (*Book of Jack London*, I, 337.) It should be compared with "Goliah," entry 127. Philip S. Foner, in *Jack London, American Rebel* (New York: The Citadel Press, 1964, p. 46), says the story is revealing of London's limitations as a socialist thinker. And, Arthur Calder-Marshall cites the story as an example of London's pioneering the "political fable" in America. See *The Bodley Head Jack London* (London: The Bodley Head, 1963), I, 8.

46. "The God of His Fathers" — *McClure's Magazine*, v. 17 (May 1901), 44-53. [GHF]

This is an oddly violent story — perhaps the most violent in all of London's fiction — with moments of great descriptive beauty: "From an island on the breast of the Yukon a colony of wild fowl voiced its interminable wrongs, while a loon laughed mockingly back across a still stretch of river." The story was the basis of a one-act play of the same name, written by David Kimball in 1910.

47. "Chris Farrington: Able Seaman" — *The Youth's Companion*, v. 75 (May 23, 1901), 265-266. [DC]

This is clearly an autobiographical story: Chris's ship is the *Sophie Sutherland* and Chris is Jack London. It is interesting to note that the tale contains, with slightly different wording, the opening lines of London's most famous short story — "To Build a Fire," (entry 108).

---

2. *The God of His Fathers and Other Stories* — New York: McClure, Phillips & Co., May, 1901. [GHF]

---

48. "A Hyperborean Brew" — *Metropolitan Magazine* (New York), v. 14 (July 1901), 85-96. [FM]

49. "Bald Face" — *The* (Oakland High School) *Aegis*, v. 22 (September 6, 1901), 1-2. [DC]

Charmian London cites this story as first appearing in *The News* in December, 1900 (*Book of Jack London*, II, 339), but *The Aegis* is the first appearance this study has found. *The News* could apply, of course, to hundreds of newspapers in the U. S. and Britain.

1902

50. "Keesh, Son of Keesh" — *Ainslee's Magazine*, v. 8 (January 1902), 526-532. [CF]

In this story, the Tana-Naw chief Gnob's dog is named "White Fang."

51. "To Build a Fire" — *The Youth's Companion*, v. 76 (May 29, 1902), 275. [Unc.]

This is the original version of the later, famed, *Century* story, (entry 108). This version was reprinted as "Never Travel Alone," in *C. B. Fry's Magazine*, 4 (February 1906), pp. 441-445. An interesting discussion of this singular episode of the two "To Build a Fire" tales, together with a printing of this first version, may be found in Earle Labor and King Hendricks, "Jack London's Twice-Told Tale," *Studies in Short Fiction*, 4 (Summer 1967), pp. 334-347. See also King Hendricks, *Jack London: Master Craftsman of the Short Story* (Logan, Utah: Utah State University, 1966), pp. 11-19.

52. "An Adventure in the Upper Sea" — *The Independent* (New York), v. 54 (May 29, 1902), 1290-1292. [DC]

53. "Diable — A Dog" — *The Cosmopolitan*, v. 33 (June 1902), 218-226. [FM]

This tale became "Bâtard" in 1904 when included in FM. The same story, with minor changes, was also called "Bâtard" when it appeared in the *Sunday Illustrated Magazine of the* (Memphis, Tenn.) *Commercial Appeal*, September 28, 1913, pp. 7-11.

54. "To Repel Boarders" — *St. Nicholas*, v. 29 (June 1902), 675-679. [DC]

---

3. *The Cruise of the Dazzler* — Complete in *St. Nicholas*, v. 29 (July 1902), 784-812.

Book publication: New York, The Century Co., October, 1902. The chief significance of this juvenile novel is that it is widely considered to be London's rarest first edition today.

---

55. "The 'Fuzziness' of Hoockla-Heen" — *The Youth's Companion*, v. 76 (July 3, 1902), 333-334. See Note.

While not included in a collection until recent times, this tale can be found in *Jack London Stories*, New York: Platt & Munk, 1960, pp. 273-286. There is a striking similarity between this story and "Li-Wan, the Fair," (entry 58).

56. "Moon-Face" — *The* (San Francisco) *Argonaut*, v. 51 (July 21, 1902), 36. [MF]

A fascinating discussion of the fact that London's "Moon-Face" and Frank

Norris' "The Passing of Cock-Eye Blacklock" both appeared in July, 1902, and both utilized a plot device involving a dog retrieving a stick of dynamite, is found in Franklin Walker's "Frank Norris and Jack London," *Mills College Magazine* (Spring 1966), pp. 15-23.

57. "Nam-Bok, the Liar" — *Ainslee's Magazine*, v. 10 (August 1902), 29-37. [CF]
This story was reprinted as "Nam-Bok, the Unveracious" in CF and in other later collections.

58. "Li-Wan, the Fair" — *The Atlantic Monthly*, v. 90 (August 1902), 212-221. [CF]
A tale very similar to "The 'Fuzziness' of Hoockla-Heen," (entry 55) and rather too close for comfort to its publication.

59. "The Master of Mystery" — *Out West* (Los Angeles), v. 17 (September 1902), 330-339. [CF]

60. "In the Forests of the North" — *Pearson's Magazine*, v. 14 (September 1902), 874-884. [CF]

61. "The Sunlanders" — September, 1902. [CF]

62. "The Death of Ligoun" — September, 1902. [CF]

4. *Children of the Frost* — New York: The Macmillan Co., September, 1902. [CF]

63. "The Story of Jees Uck" — *The Smart Set*, v. 8 (September 1902), 57-70. [FM]

5. *A Daughter of the Snows* — New York: J. B. Lippincott Co., October, 1902.
This first novel is a plodding work but important in the development of the still-maturing writer. According to Irving Stone, *McClure's* backed the book, sending the author $125 a month while he was at work on it; but upon its completion, decided against publishing it and sold the novel to Lippincott's for an advance against royalties of $750. (*Sailor on Horseback*, pp. 148, 152.) Stone says the book exemplifies London's two main weaknesses as a writer: ". . . his conception of the supremacy of the Anglo-Saxon race; and his inability to transcribe to a flesh-and-blood reality on the printed page any woman above the working class." (*Sailor on Horseback*, p. 150.)

64. "The Sickness of Lone Chief" — *Out West*, v. 17 (October 1902), 468-475. [CF]

65. "The League of the Old Men" — *Brandur Magazine* (New York), v. 1 (October 4, 1902), 7-11. [CF]

"Though the 'League of the Old Men' has no love-motif, that is not my reason for thinking it my best story," London wrote to *Grand Magazine*, 1 (August 1906), p. 86. "In ways, the motif of this story is greater than any love-motif; in fact, its wide sweep includes the conditions and situations for ten-thousand love-motifs. The voices of millions are in the voice of Old Imber, the tears and sorrows of millions in his throat as he tells his story; and his story epitomises the whole vast tragedy of the contact of the Indian with the white man. In conclusion, I may say that nobody else agrees with me in the selection which I have made and which has been my selection for years."

1903

66. "In Yeddo Bay" — *St. Nicholas*, v. 30 (February 1903), 292-296. [DC]
See entry 3.

67. "The One Thousand Dozen" — *The National Magazine* (Boston), v. 17 (March 1903), 703-713. [FM]

A tale similar to the Smoke Bellew story "A Flutter in Eggs," (entry 165), a true exploit of "Swiftwater Bill" Gates, a Klondiker of legendary fame.

68. "The Shadow and the Flash" — *The Bookman* (New York), v. 17 (June 1903), 410-417. [MF]

Charles Walcutt has observed that London ". . . increasingly moved too far away from the representative concerns of man into the realms of fantasy." See Walcutt's *Jack London* (Minneapolis: The University of Minnesota Press, Pamphlets on American Writers, No. 57, 1966), p. 28. Walcutt cites MF, entry **12**, as an example of a collection of such stories. Actually London wrote some first rate science fiction and fantasy fiction, though these stories are little-known. "The Red One" (entry 182) is probably the supreme example.

69. "The Faith of Men" — *Sunset Magazine* (San Francisco), v. 11 (June 1903), [103a], 114-121. [FM]

---

6. *The Call of the Wild* — Serialized in *The Saturday Evening Post*, June 20-July 18, 1903.

Book publication: New York, The Macmillan Co., July, 1903. Philip Foner says the book sold 10,000 copies on the first day of sale and by 1964 had sold six *million* copies. (Foner, *Jack London, American Rebel*, p. 54.)

In a letter to George P. Brett of Macmillan (March 10, 1903), London wrote, "I did not like the title, *The Call of the Wild*, and neither did the *Saturday*

Evening Post. I racked my brains for a better title & suggested *The Sleeping Wolf.* They, however, if in the meantime they do not hit upon a better title, are going to publish it in the *Post* under *The Wolf.* This I do do not like so well as *The Sleeping Wolf,* which I do not like very much either. There is a good title somewhere, if we can only lay hold of it." (*Letters,* p. 150.) Fortunately no one could lay hold of a better one so the original title was used by both the *Post* and Macmillan. The *Post* paid London $2,000 for the story and Brett offered him a flat $2,000 for outright sale of the book rights, instead of contracting for it on a royalty basis. London, to his later great disadvantage (this book alone could nearly have earned him a living for his remaining years), snapped up Brett's offer.

On March 13, 1903, London wrote to Anna Strunsky (with whom he collaborated on *The Kempton-Wace Letters* published the following May by Macmillan), "I started it as a companion to my other dog-story 'Bâtard,' which you may remember; but it got away from me, and instead of 4000 words it ran 32,000 before I could call a halt." (*Book of Jack London,* I, 388.)

This is, of course, London's supreme achievement as a story-teller, and it remains one of the very great short novels in America's literature. (See also entry 36.)

---

70. "The Leopard Man's Story" — *Frank Leslie's Popular Monthly,* v. 56 (August 1903), 408-409. [MF]

71. "The Marriage of Lit-Lit" — *Frank Leslie's Popular Monthly,* v. 56 (September 1903), 461-468. [FM]

72. "Local Color" — *Ainslee's,* v. 12 (October 1903), 74-82. [MF]

    Frederick Feied states that the ideas in this thin tale were "far better expressed in 'The Tramp,' which was published some four months later." (Feied, *No Pie in the Sky, The Hobo as American Cultural Hero in the Works of Jack London, John Dos Passos, and Jack Kerouac.* New York: The Citadel Press, 1964, p. 33.)

73. "Too Much Gold" — *Ainslee's,* v. 12 (December 1903), 109-117. [FM]

74. "Amateur Night" — *The Pilgrim* (Battle Creek, Marshall, Detroit, Mich.), v. 7 (December 1903), 5-6, 37. [MF]

1904

75. "Keesh, the Bear Hunter" — *Holiday Magazine for Children,* v. 1 (January 1904), 163-167. [LL]

    This story is often reprinted (as in LL) as "The Story of Keesh."

---

7. *The Sea Wolf* — Serialized in *The Century Magazine,* January-November, 1904.

    Book publication: New York, The Macmillan Co., October, 1904. George Brett of Macmillan was so excited over *The Sea Wolf* that he sent it to the editor of *Century*, who paid $4,000 for serial rights if given the right to blue-pencil the latter half of the novel in which Humphrey Van Weyden and Maud Brewster are left alone on an island – in 1904 a situation sure to produce palpitations in all lady readers. The novel sold 40,000 copies before its release. When London went to Manchuria to report on the Russo-Japanese War, the proofs of the novel were entrusted to his poet friend George Sterling.

Walcutt has observed that the novel takes on a decidedly different turn with the appearance of Maud Brewster: ". . . the reason may be that it corresponded with a turning point in London's life. When he was halfway through writing the book in 1903, he deserted Bess [his first wife] for Charmian Kittredge. Charmian, gushy, flirtatious, an intellectual chatterbox with a fine seat on a horse and an energetic social gaity, set her traps for London and snared him." (Walcutt, *Jack London*, p. 26.)

Franklin Walker says, "Much of *The Sea Wolf*, one of the world's great sea novels, was written aboard a trim thirty-foot sloop named *Spray*, which London had bought with part of the two thousand dollars he had just received from *The Call of the Wild*. With a cabin big enough to serve as a galley and to sleep two, London made week-long trips up San Francisco Bay and the Sacramento Delta, turning out his fifteen hundred words a day sitting on the hatch in the spring sunshine. In March, 1904, almost a year later, while the novel was appearing serially in *The Century Magazine*, its adventuresome twenty-eight-year old author was nearly freezing in an open Japanese sampan, making his way up the west coast of Korea in sub-zero weather marked by squalls alternating with treacherous calms." (Franklin Walker, Introduction to *The Sea Wolf*. New York: Signet Books, 1964), p. 377.

A good recent edition of the novel is that issued by Houghton Mifflin Co. (Riverside Edition), edited by Matthew Bruccoli, 1964.

---

76. "The Banks of the Sacramento" – *The Youth's Companion*, v. 78 (March 17, 1904), 129-130. [DC]

---

8. *The Faith of Men and Other Stories* – New York: The Macmillan Co., April, 1904. [FM]

1905

77. "White and Yellow" – *The Youth's Companion*, v. 79 (February 16, 1905), 73-74. [TFP]

To the Corresponding Editor of *The Youth's Companion*, on March 9, 1903, London wrote: "The way we captured the big Chinese fleet of shrimp-fishers in the first story 'White and Yellow' [is] again almost a literal narrative of what actually happened, even to the refusal of the Chinese to bail the *Reindeer* until she was just about ready to sink." (*Letters*, p. 147.)

78. "The King of the Greeks" – *The Youth's Companion*, v. 79 (March 2, 1905), 97-98. [TFP]

79. "A Raid on the Oyster Pirates" — *The Youth's Companion*, v. 79 (March 16, 1905), 121-122. [TFP]

80. "The Siege of the 'Lancashire Queen'" — *The Youth's Companion*, v. 79 (March 30, 1905), 149-150. [TFP]

---

9. *The Game* — Serialized in *Metropolitan Magazine*, v. 22 (April 1905), 1-8; v. 22 (May 1905), 181-193; *The Tatler* (London), v. 16 (April 5, 1905), 12, 14; v. 16 (April 12, 1905), 52, 54; v. 16 (April 19, 1905), 92, 94; v. 16 (April 26, 1905), 132, 134.

Book publication: New York, The Macmillan Co., June, 1905. Critics condemned this novelette as trivial and unbelievable, and London, disproving the latter charge at least, sent them news clippings to prove that a boxer could smash in the back of his skull by falling to the mat from a hard blow. Furthermore, London said that the lightweight champion of the world, Jimmy Britt, liked the story "on account of its trueness to life." (*Book of Jack London*, II, 10-11.)

---

81. "Charley's Coup" — *The Youth's Companion*, v. 79 (April 13, 1905), 173-74. [TFP]

82. "Demetrios Contos" — *The Youth's Companion*, v. 79 (April 27, 1905), 201-202. [TFP]

83. "'Yellow Handkerchief'" — *The Youth's Companion*, v. 79 (May 11, 1905), 225-226. [TFP]

---

10. *Tales of the Fish Patrol* — New York: The Macmillan Co., September, 1905. [TFP]

---

84. "All Gold Cañon" — *The Century Magazine*, v. 71 (November 1905), 117-127. [MF]

85. "The Sun Dog Trail" — *Harper's Monthly Magazine*, v. 112 (December 1905), 83-91. [LL]

86. "Love of Life" — *McClure's Magazine*, v. 26 (December 1905), 144-158; *Blackwood's Magazine* (Edinburgh), v. 178 (December 1905), 765-780. [LL]

The plagiarism issue touched off by the publication of this story is dealt with, among several sources, in Franklin Walker's *Jack London and the Klondike*, pp. 245-246. The story, which Lenin praised so highly, was based on the experiences

of one Charles Bunn in 1900. Bunn's ordeal was written up by two journalists
and appeared in *McClure's Magazine* the next year as "Lost in the Land of the
Midnight Sun."

1906

87. "A Nose for the King" — *The Black Cat,* v. 11 (March 1906), 1-6.
    [WGL]

"It may interest you that I've won a *Black Cat* prize — a minor prize, for it was a
skit, written, typed, and sent off in one day," London wrote to George Brett on
December 8, 1904. (*Letters,* p. 167.) He wrote Cloudesley Johns that the story of
Yi Chin Ho was told him by a Korean. (*Book of Jack London,* II, 13.)

---

11. *White Fang* — Serialized in *The Outing Magazine,* May-October,
    1906.

Book publication of *White Fang:* New York, The Macmillan Co., October, 1906.
A good recent appraisal of this novel is "Le Milieu, Le Moment, La Race:
Literary Naturalism in Jack London's *White Fang,*" by Earl Wilcox. (*Jack
London Newsletter* [Carbondale, Illinois], May-August, 1970), pp. 42-55. See
also Earle Labor, "Jack London's Mondo Cane: *The Call of the Wild* and *White
Fang,*" in *Jack London Newsletter,* (July-December, 1967), pp. 2-13.

---

88. "Planchette" — *Cosmopolitan Magazine,* v. 41 (June 1906), [122],
    157-165; v. 41 (July 1906), 259-266; v. 41 (August 1906), 378-
    386. [MF]

Maxwell Geismar says this story was "another egocentric self-portrait," and that
it is "interesting as personal history which was probably based on the break-up
of his first marriage." See Geismar's *Rebels and Ancestors: The American Novel,
1890-1915.* (Boston: Houghton Mifflin Co., 1953), p. 180. A planchette is the
triangular pointer used on a Ouija board.

89. "The Unexpected" — *McClure's Magazine,* v. 27 (August 1906), 368-
    382; *Blackwood's Magazine,* v. 180 (August 1906), 164-180. [LL]

In a letter (August 2, 1906) to the editor of the *Seattle Post-Intelligencer,*
London defends this story's basis in fact. The author said it was based on a
newspaper story from the San Francisco *Examiner* of October 14, 1900 — an
account of a double murder committed by one Michael Dennin and of Dennin's
subsequent hanging at the hands of Mr. and Mrs. Hans Nelson. London used
these names in the story. (*Jack London and the Klondike,* pp. 242-245; *Letters,*
pp. 207-208.)

90. "Brown Wolf" — *Everybody's Magazine* (New York), v. 15 (August
    1906), 147-156. [LL]

Charmian London says she suggested the idea for this story, based on London's
own Alaskan wolf-dog "Brown," whose former master was a Klondiker. (*Book
of Jack London,* II, 27-28.)

12. *Moon-Face and Other Stories* — New York: The Macmillan Co., September, 1906. [MF]
See entry 68.

---

91. "The Apostate" — *Woman's Home Companion*, v. 33 (September 1906), 5-7, 49. [WGL]
Partly autobiographical, this story of the drudgery of a young boy's life in a factory and jute mill was widely reprinted as a tract against child labor.

---

13. *Before Adam* — Serialized in *Everybody's Magazine*, October, 1906-February, 1907.
Book publication: New York, The Macmillan Co., February, 1907. During the building of the *Snark*, London ordered from England many books including Stanley Waterloo's *Story of Ab* (1897) which he leaned upon heavily in writing *Before Adam*, causing later an international stir. London replied to charges of plagiarism by acknowledging his debt to *Ab*, but insisting that primitive man was in the realm of the public domain. Charmian London wrote that the novel "went into the universities of the United States as a text-book in Anthropology." (*Book of Jack London*, II, 121; *Letters*, pp. 213-215.)

---

92. "Up the Slide" — *The Youth's Companion*, v. 80 (October 25, 1906), 545; *The Pall Mall Magazine* (London), v. 38 (November 1906), 608-612. [Unc.]

93. "A Wicked Woman" — *The Smart Set*, v. 20 (November 1906), 46-51. [WGL]
London transformed this tale into a playlet which he later included in the HD collection. This play was presented before enthusiastic audiences on the Orpheum Theater Circuit in Portland, Spokane and Seattle in July, 1910.

94. "The White Man's Way" — *Sunday Magazine of the New York Tribune*, November 4, 1906, pp. 3-4. [LL]

95. "The Wit of Porportuk" — *The Times Magazine* (New York), v. 1 (December 1906), 11-25. [LF]
The author ranked this story "among my best half-dozen Alaskan short stories." He was promised $1,000 for it from *Times Magazine* but never received the money. (*Letters*, p. 207.)

1907

96. "When God Laughs" — *The Smart Set*, v. 21 (January 1907), 39-44. [WGL]
A comparison of this story with "The Chinago" (entry 120) is found in "Jack

London's *When God Laughs:* Overman, Underdog and Satire," by Stephen T. Dhondt in *Jack London Newsletter* (May-August, 1969), pp. 51-57.

97. "'Just Meat'" — *Cosmopolitan Magazine,* v. 42 (March 1907), 535-542. [WGL]

This story was the basis of two one-act plays by Richard H. Kirschner — "Afterward" (1907) and "Burglars" (1911). It was reprinted as "Pals" in *London Magazine,* 20 (April 1908), pp. 184-193.

98. "Morganson's Finish" — *Success Magazine* (New York), v. 10 (May 1907), 311-314, 371-376. [TT]

Collected as "Finis" in TT and reprinted as "The Death Trail" in *Ellery Queen's Mystery Magazine,* 33 (January 1959), pp. 47-60.

99. "Created He Them" — *The Pacific Monthly,* v. 17 (April 1907), 393-397. [WGL]

Also published as "The Turning Point" in *Windsor Magazine,* 26 (September 1907), pp. 394-400.

100. "A Day's Lodging" — *Collier's,* v. 39 (May 25, 1907), 18-21. [LL]

This story was the basis of two three-act plays by Jack London and Herbert Heron: "Gold" (1910), and "Gold" (1913.)

101. "Negore, the Coward" — September, 1907. [LL]

This tale, written expressly for the LL collection, was, according to Charmian K. London, ". . . the first story in which he employed any portion of his many-sided love for me." (*Book of Jack London,* II, 36.)

---

14. *Love of Life and Other Stories* — New York: The Macmillan Co., September, 1907. [LL]

---

102. "Chased by the Trail" — *The Youth's Companion,* v. 81 (September 26, 1907), 445-446; *The Pall Mall Magazine* (London), v. 40 (October 1907), 478-483. [Unc.]

This rare story can also be found in *The Junior Classics,* edited by Mabel Williams and Marcia Dalphin, (New York: P. F. Collier & Sons, 1938), Volume 9, pp. 138-150; and in the 1948 edition of the same book, Volume 9, pp. 110-119.

103. "The Mission of John Starhurst" — *The Bournemouth* (England) *Visitors' Directory,* December 29, 1907, p. 10. [SST]

Reprinted as "The Whale Tooth" in *Sunset,* 24 (January 1910), pp. 49-54, and in SST. The story is based on the experience of Rev. Baker of Fiji. See J. C. Furnas, *Anatomy of Paradise — Hawaii and the Islands of the South Seas,* (New York: William Sloane Associates, Inc., 1948), p. 261.

1908

104. "The Passing of Marcus O'Brien" — *The Reader* (New York), v. 11 (January 1908), 135-144. [LF]

105. "Trust" — *The Century Magazine*, v. 75 (January 1908), 441-448. [LF]
     This story also contains a description of the Dead Horse Trail. See entry 27.

15. *The Iron Heel* — New York: The Macmillan Co., February, 1908.
     Anatole France, in a 1924 introduction of a printing of this powerful novel, said: "'The Iron Heel' is the powerful name by which Jack London designates Plutocracy. . . . Alas, Jack London had that particular genius which perceives what is hidden from the common herd, and possessed a special knowledge enabling him to anticipate the future."
     W. J. Ghent's *Our Benevolent Feudalism* (1902) is an important source and inspiration for this novel.
     The book was the basis of the play "The Iron Heel" by W. G. Henry, which was produced by the Karl Marx Players in Oakland, Calif., in March and April, 1911. (*Oakland World*, March 11, 1911, p. 2; March 18, p. 1; March 25, pp. 1-3; April 15, p. 2.)

106. "That Spot" — *Sunset Magazine*, v. 20 (February 1908), 371-376. [LF]

107. "Flush of Gold" — *Grand Magazine* (London), v. 4 (April 1908), 400-408. [LF]
     See entry 28.

108. "To Build a Fire" — *The Century Magazine*, v. 76 (August 1908), 525-534. [LF]
     London explains how this story evolved from the earlier tale of the same title which appeared in *The Youth's Companion* for May 29, 1902, in *Letters*, pp. 273-274.
     This, most famous of all Jack London short stories, was written during the *Snark* voyage. *Century* paid $300 for it. London's debt to Jeremiah Lynch's *Three Years in the Klondike* (1904) is described in *Jack London and the Klondike*, pp. 255-257.
     Both the 1902 and 1908 versions of this tale are included in *Mandala: Literature for Critical Analysis*, edited by W. L. Guerin, Earle Labor, Lee Morgan and J. R. Willingham (New York: Harper & Row, 1970).
     The famous opening to "To Build a Fire" has an interesting genesis. In the 1908 tale, it is written, "Day had broken cold and gray, exceedingly cold and gray. . . ." In "Chris Farrington, Able Seaman" (entry 47), London used the line, "after interminable hours of toil, day broke broke cold and gray." In his first novel, *A Daughter of the Snows*, entry **5**, he wrote: "It was a mid-December day, clear and cold." In "The Unexpected," (entry 89), "The day of the execution broke clear and cold." In "Morganson's Finish" (entry 98), it became "Dawn broke and merged into day. It was cold and clear."

16. *Martin Eden* — Serialized in *The Pacific Monthly*, September, 1908-September, 1909.

Book publication: New York, The Macmillan Co., September, 1909. London's working title for this novel was *Success*. Serial rights were sold for $7,000.

On the flyleaf of a copy of *Martin Eden* to Upton Sinclair, London wrote: "One of my motifs, in this book, was an attack on individualism (in the person of the hero). I must have bungled, for not a single reviewer has discovered it." See Joan London, *Jack London and His Times* (Seattle: University of Washington Press, 1968), pp. 329-330.

For a valuable discussion of this famous novel, see also Franklin Walker's "Jack London, Martin Eden," *The Voice of America Forum Lectures* (American Novel Series 12), Washington, D. C., n.d., and the 1956 Holt, Rinehart and Winston edition, Introduction by Sam Baskett.

The novel was begun in Honolulu in the summer of 1907 and finished at Papeete, Tahiti, in February, 1908. Despite the failure, frustration, turmoil and confusion of the ill-fated *Snark* voyage, the original ink manuscript of this novel shows few changes — indicating the enormous power of organization and concentration London had developed.

---

109. "The Enemy of All the World" — *The Red Book Magazine*, v. 11 (October 1908), 817-827. [STST]

110. "Aloha Oe" — *Lady's Realm* (London), v. 25 [December 1908], 170-175. [HP]

See entry 117.

111. "A Curious Fragment" — *Town Topics* (New York), December 10, 1908, pp. 45-47. [WGL]

112. "Lost Face" — *The New York Herald* (Art Section), December 13, 1908, p. 7. [LF]

Charmian London says that on May 4, 1908, at Pago Pago, Samoa, she ". . . accounted some lost hours by bringing Jack's typing up to date, namely a new Klondike [sic] story, just finished, 'Lost Face.'" See Charmian London, *Voyaging in Wild Seas* (London: Mills & Boon, Ltd., n.d.), p. 251.

An extraordinary analogue to this story is documented in Arthur Sherbo's "An Analogue for 'Lost Face,'" in *Jack London Newsletter* (September-December, 1970), pp. 95-98.

1909

113. "The Dream of Debs" — *International Socialist Review*, v. 9 (January 1909), 481-489; v. 9 (February 1909), 561-570. [STST]

This story was reprinted in pamphlet form and received wide circulation in labor organizations, especially among members of the IWW (Industrial Workers of the World) after which London patterned the militant trade union which led the general strike — the *dream* of Debs.

114. "The House of Mapuhi" — *McClure's Magazine*, v. 32 (January 1909), 247-260. [SST]

115. "The Seed of McCoy" — *The Century Magazine*, v. 77 (April 1909), 898-914. [SST]

116. "Make Westing" — *Sunset*, v. 22 (April 1909), 357-360. [WGL]

117. "The Madness of John Harned" — *Lady's Realm* (London), v. 26 [May-October, 1909], 570-581. [NB]

The month and issue number for *Lady's Realm* for this story and "Aloha Oe" (entry 110) are not known. The reference librarian at the Wilson Library, University of Minnesota, writes: ". . . we are unable to give you the month and issue number for each reference; there is no separation of issues, and the pagination is continuous within each volume. No month or issue number is indicated. Volume 25 contains 736 pages and volume 26 contains 672 pages. The title page for each volume indicates that volume 25 covers the period November 1908 to April 1909, and volume 26 covers May to October 1909." Joseph Gaer, in his *Jack London, Bibliography and Biographical Data* (New York: Burt Franklin, 1970, originally published in 1934), erroneously lists this tale as having first appeared in *Everybody's Magazine*, November, 1910. The story derived from London's experience of watching a bullfight in Quito, Ecuador.

118. "South of the Slot" — *The Saturday Evening Post*, v. 181 (May 22, 1909), 3-4, 36-38. [STST]

Arthur Calder-Marshall says that "South of the Slot" shows the split in London's nature, the conflict between the call of the wild and the domestication of civilized man seen in terms not of the dogs Buck and White Fang, but of an academic sociologist and a militant trade union leader, combined in one person. See Calder-Marshall, *The Bodley Head Jack London*, I, 15.

This story was the basis of a three-act play by London and Walter H. Nichols, "The Common Man," later revised as "The Damascus Road" (1913).

119. "Good-bye, Jack" — *The Red Book Magazine*, v. 13 (June 1909), 225-240. [HP]

120. "The Chinago" — *Harper's Monthly Magazine*, v. 119 (July 1909), 233-240. [WGL]

See also entry 96. Martin Johnson says London, on April 25, 1908, read this story aloud to the *Snark* crew en route from Bora Bora to the Samoas. (*Through the South Seas with Jack London*, p. 223.)

121. "The Sheriff of Kona" — *The American Magazine*, v. 68 (August 1909), 384-391. [HP]

122. "The Heathen" — *London Magazine* (London), v. 23 (September 1909), 33-42. [SST]

A. Calder-Marshall refers to this story as "London's version of Gunga Din." (*Bodley Head Jack London*, I, 14.) Charmian London wrote that this, perhaps the most famous of her husband's South Sea tales, was finished at Penduffryn Island, Guadalcanal, Solomon Islands, in late July, 1908, after which he began work on the novel *Adventure*. (Charmian K. London. *Log of the Snark* [New York, The Macmillan Co., 1915], pp. 384-385.)

123. "A Piece of Steak" — *The Saturday Evening Post*, v. 182 (November 20, 1909), 6-8, 42-43. [WGL]

124. "Koolau the Leper" — *The Pacific Monthly*, v. 22 (December 1909), 569-578. [HP]

Based on an incident in Hawaiian history. London perhaps first heard of Koolau from Herbert Stolz on the *Snark* voyage in 1907. Koolau had killed Stolz's father, a sheriff in the famed Kalalau Valley. See A. Grove Day's *Jack London in the South Seas* (New York: Four Winds Press, 1971), pp. 80-81.

125. "Mauki" — *Hampton's Magazine* (New York), v. 23 (December 1909), 752-760. [SST]

Charmian London wrote that Jack based this story on a Solomon Island cook he met in September, 1908, on Lua-Lua, Lord Howe Island. As the *Snark* was en route from Lord Howe to Tasman, London began to write the story of Mauki's enslavement and revenge. *A Woman Among the Headhunters* (London: Mills & Boon, Ltd., n.d.), pp. 210, 224.

1910

126. "Chun Ah Chun" — *Woman's Magazine* (St. Louis), v. 21 (Spring 1910), 5-6, 38-40. [HP]

This story was finished aboard the *Snark* on May 25, 1908, near Koro Sea, Fiji Archipelago. See Charmian K. London, *A Woman Among the Headhunters*, p. 66.

127. "Goliah" — *The Bookman* (New York), v. 30 (February 1910), 620-632. [R]

Compare this unusual tale with "The Minions of Midas," (entry 45). Martin Johnson says the story was written while the *Snark* was under construction. "One day," Johnson wrote, "he [London] read me the first part of it, in which he destroyed the Japanese Navy. 'And today I destroy the American Navy,' he told me, gleefully. 'Oh, I haven't a bit of conscience when my imagination gets to working.'" This conversation, Johnson says, took place on January 12, 1907, one of the numerous aborted sailing dates of the *Snark*. (Martin Johnson, *Through the South Seas with Jack London.* New York: Dodd, Mead and Co., 1913.) pp. 17-18. Although this story reputedly appeared in *Red Magazine* (London in 1908), neither the compiler nor the researcher of this volume was able to locate copies of the short-lived *Red Magazine* for examination; therefore, the first American appearance of this story is listed chronologically.

17. *Lost Face* – New York: The Macmillan Co., March, 1910. [LF]

128. "The Terrible Solomons" – *Hampton's Magazine*, v. 24 (March 1910), 347-354. [SST]

18. *Burning Daylight* – Serialized in *The New York Herald*, June 19-August 28, 1910.

Book publication: New York, The Macmillan Co., October, 1910. This book, says London's wife, was begun in Quito, Ecuador. (*Book of Jack London*, II, 171.) See entry 44.

129. "The Unparalleled Invasion" – *McClure's Magazine*, v. 35 (July 1910), 308-315. [STST]

Arthur Calder-Marshall says this tale "was a variation of the theme of 'the Yellow Peril,' a common nightmare of the first decade of this century." (*Bodley Head Jack London*, I, 15.)

130. "Winged Blackmail" – *The Lever* (Chicago), v. 1 (September 1910), 54-57. [NB]

Franklin Walker gives this as one of fifteen plots London bought from Sinclair Lewis, presumably on March 11, 1910, along with "When the World Was Young" (entry 131) and what later became the unfinished novel *The Assassination Bureau, Ltd.*, entry **41**. Walker says it shows Lewis' preoccupation with flying, a subject which held little interest for London. Lewis' first book, which appeared the year after this story was published, was a juvenile titled *Hike and the Aeroplane*. See Franklin Walker, "Jack London's Use of Sinclair Lewis Plots, Together With a Printing of Three of the Plots," *Huntington Library Quarterly*, 17 (November 1953), pp. 59-74.

131. "When the World Was Young" – *The Saturday Evening Post*, v. 183 (September 10, 1910), 16-17, 45-49. [NB]

See entry 130. Lewis had titled this plot "The Garden Terror."

132. "The Inevitable White Man" – *The Black Cat*, v. 16 (November 1910), 1-10. [SST]

19. *Adventure* — Serialized in *The Popular Magazine* (New York), November 1, 1910-January 15, 1911.

Book publication: New York, The Macmillan Co., March, 1911.

---

133. "The Benefit of the Doubt" — *The Saturday Evening Post*, v. 183 (November 12, 1910), 9-11, 69-70. [NB]

After the death of his new-born daughter Joy, London got into a saloon brawl in Oakland near the waterfront. The false charges of drunken brawling and an apparently prejudicial and unfair trial brought about this story for which London received $750. In a letter to Churchill Williams of *SEP* (October 4, 1910), London wrote ". . . consider this letter a legal contract or agreement to same, I hereby guarantee and pledge myself to stand for and pay all damages in any way whatsoever incurred by any suit or 'come back' that anybody may bring against *The Saturday Evening Post* on account of said story." (*Letters*, p. 319.)

134. "Under the Deck Awnings" — *The Saturday Evening Post*, v. 183 (November 19, 1910), 18-19. [NB]

135. " 'Yah! Yah! Yah!' " — *Columbian Magazine* (New York), v. 3 (December 1910), 439-447. [SST]

136. "The House of Pride" — *The Pacific Monthly*, v. 24 (December 1910), 598-607. [HP]

137. "To Kill a Man" — *The Saturday Evening Post*, v. 183 (December 10, 1910), 14-15, 40. [NB]

This story was the basis of a play of the same name by Roi Cooper Megrue, which was produced in New York in 1911, and a student dramatization of the story was presented at Dartmouth College in February, 1914. It was also the basis for the play "Chicane," which was produced by The Little Theater Society of Indiana at Indianapolis, on April 15, 1916.

138. "Bunches of Knuckles" — *The New York Herald* (Art Section), December 18, 1910, pp. 2-3. [NB]

1911

139. "The 'Francis Spaight' " — January, 1911. [WGL]

---

20. *When God Laughs and Other Stories* — New York: The Macmillan Co., January, 1911. [WGL]

---

140. "The Hobo and the Fairy" — *The Saturday Evening Post*, v. 183 (February 11, 1911), 12-13, 41-42. [TT]

141. "The Strength of the Strong" — *Hampton's Magazine,* v. 26 (March 1911), 309-318. [STST]

Philip Foner writes that this tale is one of the best parables in American literature. The story was reprinted as a pamphlet by the Charles H. Kerr Co. of Chicago, the Socialist Cooperative Publishing House, and became a classic of Socialist literature. (Foner, *Jack London, American Rebel.* New York: The Citadel Press, 1947), p. 109. In a letter to *Cosmopolitan* (August 30, 1909), London wrote: "If you will remember, some time ago, Kipling made an attack on Socialism in the form of a parable or short story, entitled 'Melissa,' in which he exploited his Jingoism and showed that a co-operation of individuals strong enough to overcome war meant the degeneration of said individuals. I have written my 'Strength of the Strong' as a reply to his attack." (*Letters,* pp. 287-288.)

142. "The Eternity of Forms" — *The Red Book Magazine,* v. 16 (March 1911), 866-873. [TT]

This story was reprinted as "The Dead Do Not Come Back" in *Ellery Queen's Mystery Magazine,* 37 (February 1961), 67-76.

143. "A Son of the Sun" — *The Saturday Evening Post,* v. 183 (May 27, 1911), 18-20, 45. [SS]

144. "The Taste of the Meat" — *Cosmopolitan,* v. 51 (June 1911), 16-28. [SB]

This is the first of the Smoke Bellew tales, for each of which London received $750. Irving Stone says the series has no literary value and is London's first "hack work." In fact, London had written a good deal of hackwork before 1911 and the Smoke Bellew stories, greatly under-rated in nearly all critical appraisals of London's work, are first-rate tales. London said of them "I didn't like the job of writing the thirteen [*sic*] Smoke Bellew stories, but I never hedged from my best in writing them." *Sailor on Horseback,* pp. 296-297.) London's reference to the *thirteen* stories is probably due to the fact that "Wonder of Woman" (entry 170) was written in two parts.

It should be noted that *Smoke Bellew* is sometimes counted as a "novel" of London's although it is clearly a collection of twelve stories, each of which can stand alone, built around the Klondike adventures of Christopher Bellew.

145. "The Proud Goat of Aloysius Pankburn" — *The Saturday Evening Post,* v. 183 (June 24, 1911), 5-7, 33-36. [SS]

146. "The Meat" — *Cosmopolitan,* v. 51 (July 1911), 209-222. [SB]

147. "The Night Born" — *Everybody's Magazine,* v. 25 (July 1911), 108-117. [NB]

148. "War" — *The Nation* (London), v. 9 (July 29, 1911), 635-636. [NB]

Charmian London says her husband wrote "what he called a picture, or, rather, two successive pictures, entitled 'War,' which he deemed one of his gems; and the story 'To Kill a Man,'', which he also greatly liked." (*Book of Jack London*, II, 194.) Though little-known, "War" is surely one of London's short story classics. An interesting comparison can be made between this tale and Ambrose Bierce's earlier "An Occurrence at Owl Creek Bridge."

149. "The Goat Man of Fuatino" — *The Saturday Evening Post*, v. 184 (July 29, 1911), 12-15, 35-38. [ss]

This story appears as "The Devils of Fuatino" in SS.

150. "The Stampede to Squaw Creek" — *Cosmopolitan*, v. 51 (August 1911), 356-368. [sb]

Compare to "Thanksgiving on Slav Creek" (entry 34.)

151. "The Mexican" — *The Saturday Evening Post*, v. 184 (August 19, 1911), 6-8, 27-30. [nb]

152. "Shorty Dreams" — *Cosmopolitan*, v. 51 (September 1911), 437-446. [sb]

---

21. *The Abysmal Brute* — Complete in *The Popular Magazine* (New York), v. 21 (September 1, 1911), 1-35.

Book publication: New York, The Macmillan Co., May, 1913. The plot for this novelette was purchased by London from Sinclair Lewis on October 4, 1910, for $7.50, according to Franklin Walker. ("Jack London's Use of Sinclair Lewis Plots.") The editors of *Letters From Jack London* say London used none of the plots bought from Lewis on October 4, 1910. (*Letters*, p. 485.)
On October 20, 1911, London wrote Lewis: "Frankly I don't know whether I'm making money or losing money by working up some of those short-story ideas from you. Take *The Abysmal Brute* for instance. I got $1200.00 for it, after it had been refused by the first-class magazines. Had the time I devoted to it been devoted to some *Smoke Bellew* or *Sun Tales*, I'd have got $3000 for the same amount of work." (*Letters*, p. 488.) London also said, however, in the same letter to Lewis, "Personally, despite the fact that it did not make a financial killing, I'm darned glad I wrote *The Abysmal Brute*."

---

153. "A Little Account with Swithin Hall" — *The Saturday Evening Post*, v. 184 (September 2, 1911), 12-14, 40-41. [ss]

Of considerable interest in this David Grief story is the list of books Swithin Hall has on his island. Extrapolated, it gives a fair view of what London may have been reading in 1911.

154. "A Goboto Night" — *The Saturday Evening Post*, v. 184 (September 30, 1911), 20-21, 65-66. [ss]

For a discussion of this tale and of London's occasional use of detective story devices, see "Jack London, Sherlock Holmes and the Agent," by Dale L. Walker, in *The Baker Street Journal*, 20 (June 1970), pp. 79-85.

22. *South Sea Tales* — New York: The Macmillan Co., October, 1911. [SST]

155. "The Man on the Other Bank" — *Cosmopolitan*, v. 51 (October 1911), 677-688. [SB]

156. "The Pearls of Parlay" — *The Saturday Evening Post*, v. 184 (October 14, 1911), 9-11, 64-66. [SS]

Eugene Burdick, in his Introduction to *The Best Short Stories of Jack London* (New York: Fawcett World Library, 1967), says that in this story, London writes of a typhoon, "that most difficult of things to describe. . . . London's description is masterful, an exercise in economy and the glancing insight. . . . In the end London does the impossible: he makes the wind visible, gives it palpable character." For further evidence of this extraordinary descriptive power, one should read carefully "The Heathen" (entry 122), and "The House of Mapuhi" (entry 114), as well as the young Jack London's "Story of a Typhoon Off the Coast of Japan" (1893).

157. "The Race for Number Three" — *Cosmopolitan*, v. 51 (November 1911), 823-835. [SB]

158. "The End of the Story" — *Woman's World* (Chicago), v. 27 (November 1911), 8-9, 29-32. [TT]

Reprinted as "The Fearless One" in the *Jack London's Adventure Magazine*, 1 (October 1958), pp. 5-20. This magazine survived only the single issue.

159. "The Jokers of New Gibbon" — *The Saturday Evening Post*, v. 184 (November 11, 1911), 18-19, 65-66. [SS]

160. "By the Turtles of Tasman" — *The San Francisco Call, The Monthly Magazine*, November 19, 1911, pp. 8-10, 17-19. [TT]

161. "The Little Man" — *Cosmopolitan*, v. 52 (December 1911), 15-25. [SB]

162. "The Unmasking of the Cad" — *Monmouthshire* (England) *Weekly Post*, December 23, 1911, p. 16. [Unc.]

This little tableau was published by the Tillotson Syndicate and Charmian London gives the first publication date as July, 1899 (*Book of Jack London*, II, 398), but the present study has found no publication earlier than December 23, 1911.

1912

163. "The Hanging of Cultus George" — *Cosmopolitan Magazine*, v. 52
    (January 1912), 200-210. [SB]

164. "The Mistake of Creation" — *Cosmopolitan Magazine*, v. 52 (Febru-
    ary 1912), 335-347. [SB]

---

23. *The House of Pride & Other Tales of Hawaii* — New York: The Mac-
    millan Co., March, 1912. [HP]

---

165. "A Flutter in Eggs" — *Cosmopolitan Magazine*, v. 52 (March 1912),
    545-558. [SB]
    Compare this story to "The One Thousand Dozen" (entry 67). Wild Water
    Charley in this tale is based on real-life Klondiker "Swiftwater Bill" Gates.

166. "The Sea-Farmer" — *The Bookman* (New York), v. 35 (March 1912),
    51-60. [STST]
    See entry 173.

167. "The Feathers of the Sun" — *The Saturday Evening Post*, v. 184
    (March 9, 1912), 6-9, 72-74. [SS]

168. "The Grilling of Loren Ellery" — (Middlebrough, England) *Northern
    Weekly Gazette*, March 20, 1912, p. 9. [Unc.]
    This story was also published by the Tillotson Syndicate. A recent printing of
    this rarity may be found in *The Daily Californian Weekly Magazine* (April 4,
    1969), pp. 14, 17.

169. "The Town-Site of Tra-Lee" — *Cosmopolitan Magazine*, v. 52 (April
    1912), 701-714. [SB]

170. "Wonder of Woman" — *Cosmopolitan Magazine*, v. 52 (May 1912),
    761-773, [Part 1]; *Cosmopolitan Magazine*, v. 53 (June 1912),
    107-120, [Part 2]. [SB]
    This story was printed as a pamphlet by the International Magazine Co. (New
    York, 1912). Compare with entry 29. Mrs. London said she suggested that Jack
    continue the Smoke Bellew series, taking Smoke and Shorty into the South Seas.
    (*Book of Jack London*, II, 202.) Would that he had!

24. *A Son of the Sun* – New York: Doubleday, Page & Co., May, 1912. [ss]

Also published as *The Adventures of Captain Grief* (New York: The World Publishing Co., 1954).

171. "The Prodigal Father" – *Woman's World*, v. 28 (May 1912), 5, 29, 31-33; *The Pall Mall Magazine* (London), v. 49 (May 1912), 711-718. [tt]

This is yet another of the nine plots London purchased from Sinclair Lewis on October 4, 1910. London paid $5 for this one; the only other in the batch that he used, according to Franklin Walker, was "The Dress Suit Pugilist" which became the novelette *The Abysmal Brute*. [See entries 130, 131, and **21**].

25. *The Scarlet Plague* – Complete in *London Magazine*, v. 28 (June 1912), 513-540.

Book publication: New York, The Macmillan Co., May, 1915. Franklin Walker calls this novel ". . . perhaps the best example in American literature of a genre today very popular, the survival novel." ("Afterword" to *The Sea Wolf and Selected Stories*. New York: The New American Library, 1964, p. 346.)

26. *Smoke Bellew* – New York: The Century Co., October, 1912. [sb]

172. "The Captain of the Susan Drew" – *The San Francisco Call, The Semi-Monthly Magazine*, December 1, 1912, pp. 3-4, 9-13. [Unc.]

Reprinted with slight revisions as "Poppy Cargo" in *Physical Culture*, 66 (July 1931), pp. 17-19, 116-122, where it was billed as "the literary sensation of 1931." In this same magazine, Charmian London states that her husband wrote both "The Captain of the Susan Drew" and "Poppy Cargo" during the *Dirigo* voyage. She gives "The Tar Pot" as another name for this story. (*Book of Jack London*, II, 405.)

1913

27. *The Night-Born* – New York: The Century Co., February, 1913. [nb]

28. *John Barleycorn* – Serialized in *The Saturday Evening Post*, March 15-May 3, 1913.

Book publication: New York, The Century Co., August, 1913. This work is generally classified as an "autobiographical novel." The perceptive Arthur Calder-Marshall writes that *Barleycorn* ". . . is conceded by the few modern critics who have read it, to be 'a classic of alcoholism.' But in my view it is a literary masterpiece, not merely the greatest book which Jack London wrote, but, seen in its true setting, one of the most poignant documents of our century, a fortuitous work of inhibited and tortured genius." (*Bodley Head Jack London,* II, 7.)

29. *The Valley of the Moon* — Serialized in *Cosmopolitan,* April-December, 1913.

Book publication: New York, The Macmillan Co., October, 1913. Chapters 6-10 of Book Three of this novel form a fiction account of the Carmel colony, which Franklin Walker has chronicled in *The Seacoast of Bohemia* (San Francisco: The Book Club of California, 1966.)

173. "Samuel" — *The Bookman* (New York), v. 37 (May 1913), 285-296. [STST]

Charmian London says her husband got the inspiration for this story and "The Sea Farmer" (entry 166) from Captain Robert McIlwaine of the Scotch collier *Tymeric,* en route from Newcastle, New South Wales, to Guayaquil, Ecuador. (*Book of Jack London,* II, 174-175.) London, in a letter to John S. Phillips of *American Magazine,* dated May 26, 1910, wrote: "Why, the material in that story of 'Samuel' cost me at least $250 hard cash to acquire, and 43 days at sea between land and land, on a coal-laden tramp-steamer. Also, it took me two weeks to write. And my wife threw in 43 days of her time helping in making a study of the vernacular, and in writing it down and classifying it. How the dickens I could sell that story for $250 and make both ends meet is beyond me." (*Letters,* p. 305.)

30. *The Sea Gangsters* — Serialized in *Hearst's Magazine,* November, 1913-August, 1914.

Book publication as *The Mutiny of the Elsinore,* New York: The Macmillan Co., September, 1914.

1914

31. *The Strength of the Strong* — New York: The Macmillan Co., May, 1914. [STST]

174. "Told in the Drooling Ward" — *The Bookman* (New York), v. 39 (June 1914), 432-437. [TT]

1915

32. *The Star Rover* — Serialized in *Los Angeles Examiner, American Sunday Monthly Magazine,* February 14-October 10, 1914.

Book publication: New York, The Macmillan Co., October, 1915. Other titles London considered using with this novel were *The Jacket* (which was actually used in some British editions of the novel and in the present Horizon Edition), and *The Shirt Without a Collar*. Joan London says: *"The Star Rover,* which was completed shortly before he went to Mexico in 1914, was Jack's last attempt at a serious work. Into this extraordinary and little-known book he flung with a prodigal hand riches which he had hoarded for years, and compressed into brilliant episodes notes originally intended for full-length books. Of all his later work, only portions of this novel and a few short stories reveal the fulfillment of the artistic promise so evident in his early writings. After *The Star Rover* he made no further effort to write well." (Joan London, *Jack London and His Times.* New York: Doubleday, Doran & Co., Inc., 1939, p. 362.) A new edition of this fine study of her father's life and times was published by the University of Washington Press (Seattle) in 1968 with new introductory material by Joan London.

33. *The Little Lady of the Big House* — Serialized in *Cosmopolitan Magazine,* April, 1915-January, 1916.

Book publication: New York, The Macmillan Co., April, 1916. London thought this novel would be "a cleancut gem, even in serial form — a jewel of artistry." (*Letters,* p. 375.) For a recent evaluation of the long-neglected book, see "The Symbolic Triad in London's *The Little Lady of the Big House,"* by Edwin B. Erbentraut, *Jack London Newsletter,* (September-December, 1970), pp. 82-89.

1916

34. *The Turtles of Tasman* — New York: The Macmillan Co., September, 1916. [TT]

175. "The Hussy" — *Cosmopolitan Magazine,* v. 62 (December 1916), 18-23, 94, 97, 99. [RO]

London paid George Sterling $100 for the plot of this story. (Letter from Jack London to George Sterling, written from Honolulu, March 7, 1916, Huntington Library files.) Paying such a fee seems to confirm Mary Austin's view: "I have always suspected that Jack's buying of plots for short stories from any writer with more plots than places to bestow them was chiefly a generous camouflage for help that could not be asked or given otherwise." See Mary Austin's *Earth Horizon* (New York: The Literary Guild, 1932), p. 304.

1917

35. *Jerry of the Islands* — Serialized in *Cosmopolitan Magazine,* January-April, 1917.

Book publication: New York, The Macmillan Co., April, 1917.

176. "Man of Mine" — *Hearst's Magazine,* v. 31 (February 1917), 11, 130-134. [OMM]

Reprinted as "The Kanaka Surf" in OMM.

177. "Like Argus of the Ancient Times" — *Hearst's Magazine*, v. 31 (March 1917), 176-178, 214-216. [RO]

> Irving Stone says of this marvelous story that it shows London rearing up for a last show of strength. (*Sailor on Horseback*, p. 329.) Charmian London adds, ". . . Jack himself walks across some of the pages as young Liverpool." (*Book of Jack London*, II, 355.)
>
> Franklin Walker says London had read Jung's *Psychology of the Unconscious* (1916) when he introduced the idea of racial memory in John Tarwater's fever-dream sequence. (*Jack London and the Klondike*, p. 233.)

36. *Michael, Brother of Jerry* — Serialized in *Cosmopolitan Magazine*, May-October, 1917.

> Book publication: New York, The Macmillan Co., November, 1917. In this book, London championed the end of the training of animals for the vaudeville stage. After its publication, Jack London Clubs sprang up across the country and in Europe and, according to Joan London, "By 1924 the Jack London Clubs throughout the world had a reported membership of four hundred thousand, and in the United States at least animal acts had practically disappeared." (*Jack London and His Times*, 1968 edition, p. 363.)

1918

37. *Hearts of Three* — London: Mills & Boon, Ltd., 1918.

> First American Edition, New York: The Macmillan Co., September 1920. This "frenzied fiction" movie scenario ran as a serial in Hearst's New York *Evening Journal* between May 12 and June 20, 1919. The *Oakland Tribune* magazine section also serialized it between August 31 and December 7, 1919. No film was ever made of it.

178. "When Alice Told Her Soul" — *Cosmopolitan*, v. 64 (March 1918), 28-33, 105-107. [OMM]

179. "The Princess" — *Cosmopolitan*, v. 65 (June 1918), 20-27, 145-149. [RO]

180. "The Tears of Ah Kim" — *Cosmopolitan*, v. 65 (July 1918), 32-37, 136-138. [OMM]

181. "The Water Baby" — *Cosmopolitan*, v. 65 (September 1918), 80-85, 133. [OMM]

> Charmian London wrote that this, London's last written story, ". . . is clearly a symbolic representation of the Rebirth, the return to the Mother, exemplified by the arguments of the old Hawaiian Kohokumu." (*Book of Jack London*, II, 354.)

182. "The Red One" — *Cosmopolitan*, v. 65 (October 1918), 34-41, 132, 135-138. [RO]

In a letter to Upton Sinclair dated October 10, 1931, Charmian London wrote that the "suggestion of the great, round, possibly-meteorite" came from London's friend, the poet George Sterling. (*Jack London Newsletter*, January-April, 1971, p. 43). The playlet "The First Poet" (in TT), and "The Hussy" (entry 175) were other London-Sterling collaborations.

38. *The Red One* — New York: The Macmillan Co., October, 1918. [RO]

183. "In the Cave of the Dead" — *Cosmopolitan*, v. 65 (November 1918), 74-81, 119-121. [OMM]

Reprinted as "Shin-Bones" in OMM.

1919

184. "On the Makaloa Mat" — *Cosmopolitan*, v. 66 (March 1919), 16-23, 133-135. [OMM]

185. "The Bones of Kahekili" — *Cosmopolitan*, v. 67 (July 1919), 95-100, 102, 104. [OMM]

39. *On the Makaloa Mat* — New York: The Macmillan Co., September 1919. [OMM]

1922

186. "Whose Business Is to Live" — September, 1922. [DC]

40. *Dutch Courage and Other Stories* — New York: The Macmillan Co., September, 1922. [DC]

1924

187. "Eyes of Asia" — *Cosmopolitan Magazine*, v. 77 (September 1924), 24-31, 148, 150-156. [Unc.]

This story represents part of a novel London was writing at the time of his death on November 22, 1916. He called the work-in-progress *Cherry*. (*Letters*, p. 474.) The story was completed by Charmian K. London. See her "How Jack London Would Have Ended 'Eyes of Asia,'" *Cosmopolitan Magazine*, 77 (October 1924), 78-79, 124, 126, 128, 130-131. Significantly, this story, never reprinted in English, has appeared twice in Russian translation. (See Woodbridge, London, Tweney, *Jack London: A Bibliography*, pp. 186, 189.)

1926

188. "A Northland Miracle" — *The Youth's Companion,* v. 100 (November
    4, 1926), 813-814. [Unc.]

John Thornton of *The Call of the Wild* is one of the main characters in this
heretofore unlisted story.

1963

41. *The Assassination Bureau, Ltd.* — New York: McGraw-Hill Book Co.,
    Inc., 1963.

This novel was unfinished at London's death. It had been sent to *The Saturday
Evening Post* in December, 1911, in unfinished (about 30,000 words completed) form. (*Letters,* p. 357.) It is one of the Sinclair Lewis plots and was
given an ending by mystery story writer Robert L. Fish "from notes by Jack
London." These notes, along with others, are contained at the end of the
McGraw-Hill edition, but Fish obviously made little use of them — and it is
perhaps best that he didn't. London purchased the plot for the story from Lewis
on March 11, 1910. It was one of five plots he actually used from a total of
twenty-seven he bought from Lewis for a total sum of $137.50. This one is the
only real novel that resulted from this "collaboration." The plot "The Dress-
Suit Pugilist" became the novelette *The Abysmal Brute,* entry **21**, and three
others became short stories, all of them exceedingly bad. (See Mark Schorer,
Sinclair Lewis, An American Life. New York: McGraw-Hill Co., Inc., 1961, pp.
164-166; also Franklin Walker's "Jack London's Use of Sinclair Lewis Plots;"
and *Letters,* pp. 483-489.) Refer also to entries 130, 131, **21**, and 171.

THE BOOKS OF JACK LONDON: A CHRONOLOGY

The Son of the Wolf	Boston: Houghton, Mifflin and Co.	April 7	1900
The God of His Fathers & *Other Stories*	New York: McClure, Phillips & Co.	May	1901
Children of the Frost	New York: The Macmillan Co.	September	1902
The Cruise of the Dazzler	New York: The Century Co.	October	1902
A Daughter of the Snows	New York: J. B. Lippincott Co.	October	1902
The Kempton-Wace Letters	New York: The Macmillan Co.	May	1903
The Call of the Wild	New York: The Macmillan Co.	July	1903
The People of the Abyss	New York: The Macmillan Co.	October	1903
The Faith of Men & *Other Stories*	New York: The Macmillan Co.	April	1904
The Sea Wolf	New York: The Macmillan Co.	October	1904
War of the Classes	New York: The Macmillan Co.	April	1905
The Game	New York: The Macmillan Co.	June	1905
Tales of the Fish Patrol	New York: The Macmillan Co.	September	1905
Moon-Face & *Other Stories*	New York: The Macmillan Co.	September	1906
White Fang	New York: The Macmillan Co.	October	1906
Scorn of Women	New York: The Macmillan Co.	November	1906
Before Adam	New York: The Macmillan Co.	February	1907
Love of Life & *Other Stories*	New York: The Macmillan Co.	September	1907
The Road	New York: The Macmillan Co.	November	1907
The Iron Heel	New York: The Macmillan Co.	February	1908
Martin Eden	New York: The Macmillan Co.	September	1909
Lost Face	New York: The Macmillan Co.	March	1910
Revolution & *Other Essays*	New York: The Macmillan Co.	March	1910
Burning Daylight	New York: The Macmillan Co.	October	1910
Theft	New York: The Macmillan Co.	November	1910
When God Laughs & *Other Stories*	New York: The Macmillan Co.	January	1911
Adventure	New York: The Macmillan Co.	March	1911
The Cruise of the Snark	New York: The Macmillan Co.	June	1911
South Sea Tales	New York: The Macmillan Co.	October	1911
The House of Pride & *Other Tales of Hawaii*	New York: The Macmillan Co.	March	1912
A Son of the Sun	New York: Doubleday, Page & Co.	May	1912
Smoke Bellew	New York: The Century Co.	October	1912
The Night-Born	New York: The Century Co.	February	1913
The Abysmal Brute	New York: The Century Co.	May	1913
John Barleycorn	New York: The Century Co.	August	1913
The Valley of the Moon	New York: The Macmillan Co.	October	1913
The Strength of the Strong	New York: The Macmillan Co.	May	1914
The Mutiny of the Elsinore	New York: The Macmillan Co.	September	1914
The Scarlet Plague	New York: The Macmillan Co.	May	1915
The Star Rover	New York: The Macmillan Co.	October	1915
The Acorn Planter	New York: The Macmillan Co.	February	1916
The Little Lady of the Big House	New York: The Macmillan Co.	April	1916
*The Turtles of Tasman*****	New York: The Macmillan Co.	September	1916
The Human Drift	New York: The Macmillan Co.	February	1917
Jerry of the Islands	New York: The Macmillan Co.	April	1917
Michael, Brother of Jerry	New York: The Macmillan Co.	November	1917
The Red One	New York: The Macmillan Co.	October	1918
Hearts of Three	London: Mills & Boon, Ltd.		1918
	New York: The Macmillan Co.	September	1920
On the Makaloa Mat	New York: The Macmillan Co.	September	1919
Dutch Courage & *Other Stories*	New York: The Macmillan Co.	September	1922
The Assassination Bureau, Ltd.	New York: McGraw-Hill Books		1963
Letters from Jack London	New York: The Odyssey Press		1965
(Edited by King Hendricks and Irving Shepard.)			
Jack London Reports	Garden City: Doubleday & Co.		1970
(Edited by King Hendricks and Irving Shepard.)			

*The last book published in Jack London's lifetime.

JACK LONDON: A CHRONOLOGY

1876   Born at 615 Third Street, San Francisco, California, January 12. Son
       of Flora Wellman (born Massillon, Ohio, August 17, 1843) and
       William Henry Chaney (born near present-day Chesterville, Maine,
       January 13, 1821). Chaney, an itinerant astrologer, lived with Flora
       Wellman during 1874-1875. Chaney deserted his common-law wife
       upon learning of her pregnancy and later (1897) denied to London
       that he could have been his father.
       On September 7, Flora (who used the name Chaney) marries John
       London, a native of Pennsylvania and Union Army veteran, a wid-
       ower with two daughters. John London accepts Flora's son as his
       own and he is named John Griffith London, the middle name deriv-
       ing from a favorite nephew of Flora Wellman's, Griffith Everhard.

1891   Completes grammar school. Works in a cannery.

1892   Purchases the sloop *Razzle-Dazzle* with $300 borrowed from his
       former wet nurse "Mammy Jenny" Prentiss and becomes "Prince of
       the Oyster Pirates" on San Francisco Bay.
       Serves as officer in the Fish Patrol on San Francisco Bay.

1893   Serves several months aboard the sealing schooner *Sophie Suther-
       land* in Bering Sea sealing waters and the North Pacific. Returns in
       summer and on November 12, wins first prize in the San Francisco
       Call's "Best Descriptive Article" contest for "Story of a Typhoon Off
       the Coast of Japan."

1894   Joins the western detachment of "Coxey's Army," — "Kelly's Army"—
       to march to Washington, D.C. Leaves the ragtag "army" in the Mid-
       west and rides the rails eastward. Is arrested for vagrancy in Niagara
       Falls, N.Y. in June and serves one month in the Erie County Peniten-
       tiary. These experiences he will later chronicle in *The Road* (1907).

1895   Finishes public school education at Oakland High School where he
       writes sketches and stories for the student magazine *Aegis*.

1896   Joins Socialist Labor Party. Passes entrance examinations and at-
       tends the University of California at Berkeley for one semester.

1897   Joins Klondike gold rush and spends the winter in the Yukon.
       John London dies in Oakland on October 14.

1898   Returns from Alaska via 2,000 mile boat trip down the Yukon River.

1899   Publishes first "professional" story, "To the Man on the Trail" in
       Overland Monthly. Begins writing for a living.

December 21, signs contract with Houghton, Mifflin & Co. for a book of short stories.

1900 "An Odyssey of the North" is published in *The Atlantic Monthly.* Marries Bessie Maddern on April 7; on the same day, his first published book, *The Son of the Wolf,* a collection of Northland fiction, appears.

1901 First daughter, Joan, is born.

1902 Travels to London where he lives six weeks in the city's East End ghetto, and there gathers material for his brilliant sociological study, *The People of the Abyss* (a phrase credited to H. G. Wells.)
Second daughter, Bess, is born.
First novel, *A Daughter of the Snows,* is published by Lippincott's.

1903 W. H. Chaney dies on January 8.
The Kempton-Wace Letters, an epistolary exchange with co-author Anna Strunsky on the subject of love, is published by Macmillan.
Separates from Bessie London.
The Call of the Wild is published, an instantaneous success.

1904 Sails for Japan and Korea as war correspondent for the Hearst Syndicate in the Russo-Japanese War.
The Sea Wolf is published, London's second most famous novel.

1905 Divorces Bessie Maddern London. Marries Charmian Kittredge on November 20 in Chicago.
Purchases ranch near Glen Ellen, California.
Lectures in Midwest and East.

1906 Lectures at Yale in January on "The Coming Crisis."
Reports on the San Francisco earthquake and fire, April 18, for *Collier's.* Begins building the *Snark* (named after Lewis Carroll's creation), to sail around the world.
White Fang, written as a companion volume to *The Call of the Wild,* is published.

1907 Sails April 23 from San Francisco in *Snark,* visiting Hawaii — including the leper colony at Molokai —, the Marquesas, and Tahiti.

1908 Returns to California aboard the *Mariposa* to straighten out financial affairs. Continues *Snark* voyage to Samoa, Fiji Islands, New Hebrides, and the Solomon Islands.
The Iron Heel is published.

1909 Is hospitalized in Sydney, Australia, with a series of tropical ail-

ments. Abandons *Snark* voyage and returns to California on the
Scotch collier *Tymeric* via Pitcairn Island, Ecuador, Panama, New
Orleans and Arizona.
Arrives at Wake Robin Lodge on July 24.
Martin Eden, a semi-autobiographical novel, is published.

1910 Devotes energies, and funds, to building up his "Beauty Ranch."
Wolf House, London's baronial mansion, is begun.
Birth and death of the Londons' first child, a daughter named Joy.

1911 With his wife and servant, drives a four-horse carriage through
northern California and Oregon.

1912 Sails on March 2 from Baltimore around Cape Horn to Seattle
aboard the four-masted barque *Dirigo*, a 148-day voyage.
The Londons' second baby lost in miscarriage.

1913 Wolf House, on August 21 is mysteriously destroyed by fire, a
$70,000 loss, probably arson.
John Barleycorn, semi-autobiographical novel-treatise on alcoholism, is published..

1914 Becomes correspondent for *Collier's*, at $1100 a week, in Mexican
Revolution.

1915 Returns to Hawaii, this time for health purposes.
His last great work, *The Star Rover*, is published.
Is warned by doctors of his excesses in drink and diet.

1916 Resigns from Socialist Party "because of its lack of fire and fight, and
its loss of emphasis on the class struggle."
Dies at 7:45 p.m., November 22, of uremic poisoning. Suicide, as
suggested by biographical novelist Irving Stone (in *Sailor on Horseback*), by a calculated lethal dose of morphine and atropine sul-
phates, a possibility but in no way conclusive.

1922 Flora Wellman London dies on January 4.

1947 Bess Maddern London dies on September 7.

1955 Charmian Kittredge London dies on January 13.

1965 *Letters from Jack London*, most important of all source books on
London's life and thought, is published by Odyssey Press, edited by
King Hendricks and Irving Shepard.

1970 *Jack London Reports*, a collection of London's war correspondence,
prize-fight reporting and miscellaneous newspaper writing, is published by Doubleday, edited by King Hendricks and Irving Shepard.

1971 Joan London dies on January 18.

● *George Sterling, Jack London, and Porter Garnett at the Bohemian Grove. Sterling (1870-1926) collaborated with London on at least two stories (see entries 175 and 182) and a short play. Porter Garnett (1871-1951) was a San Francisco-born author of* THE BOHEMIAN JINKS *(1908),* THE GREEN KNIGHT *(1911), and other works. He also was producer of Grove plays for the San Francisco Bohemian Club, and was a teacher of "fine printing" at Carnegie Institute of Technology from 1922 to 1935, where one of the students upon whom he "left his mark" was J. Carl Hertzog, designer of this book.*

● *Jack and Charmian London in front of his Wake Robin Lodge, near Glen Ellen, California. (Photos courtesy of The Bancroft Library.)*

THE REJUVENATION OF MAJOR RATHBONE

By Jack London

Drawing by Louis Betts

ALCHEMY was a magnificent dream, fascinating, impossible; but before it passed away there sprang from its loins a more marvelous child, none other than chemistry. More marvelous, because it substituted fact for fancy, and immensely widened man's realm of achievement. It has turned probability into possibility, and from the ideal it has fashioned the real. Do you follow me?"

Dover absently hunted for a match, at the same time regarding me with a heavy seriousness which instantly called to my mind Old Doc Frawley, our clinical lecturer of but a few years previous. I nodded assent, and he, having appropriately wreathed himself in smoke, went on with his discourse.

"Alchemy has taught us many things, while not a few of its visions have been realized by us in these latter days. The Elixir of Life was absurd, perpetual youth a rank negation of the very principle of life. But —"

Dover here paused with exasperating solemnity.

* * *

"But prolongation of life is too common an incident nowadays for any one to question. Not so very long ago, a 'generation' represented thirty-three years, the average duration of human existence. To-day, because of the rapid strides of medicine, sanitation, distribution, and so forth, a 'generation' is reckoned at thirty-four years. By the time of our great-grandchildren, it may have increased to forty years. Quien sabe? And again, we ourselves may see it actually doubled."

"Ah!" he cried, observing my start. "You see what I am driving at?"

"Yes," I replied. "But —"

"Never mind the 'buts,' " he burst in autocratically. "You ossified conservatives have always hung back at the coat-tails of science —"

"And as often saved it from breaking its neck," I retaliated.

"Just hold your horses a minute, and let me go on. What is life? Schopenhauer has defined it as the affirmation of the will to live, which is a philosophical absurdity, by the way, but with which we have no concern. Now, what is death? Simply the wearing out, the exhaustion, the breaking down, of the cells, tissues, nerves, bones and muscles of the human organism. Surgeons find great difficulty in knitting the broken bones of elderly people. Why? Because the bone, weakened, approaching the stage of dissolution, is no longer able to cast off the mineral deposits thrust in upon it by the natural functions of the body. And how easily such a bone is fractured! Yet, were it possible to remove the large deposits of phosphate, carbonate of soda, and so forth, the bone would regain the spring and rebound which it possessed in its youth.

"MORNING AFTER MORNING HE COULD BE SEEN TRAMPING HOME FOR BREAKFAST ACROSS THE DEWY FIELDS"

"Merely apply this process, in varying measures, to the rest of the anatomy, and you have what? Simply the retardation of the system's break-up, the circumvention of old age, the banishment of senility, and the recapture of giddy youth. If science has prolonged the life of the generation by one year, is it not equally possible that it may prolong that of the individual by many?"

To turn back the dial of life, to reverse the hour-glass of Time and run its golden sands anew —the audacity of it fascinated me. What was to prevent? If one year, why not twenty? Forty?

Pshaw! I was just beginning to smile at my credulity when Dover pulled open the drawer beside him and brought to view a metal-stoppered vial. I confess to a sharp pang of disappointment as I gazed upon the very ordinary liquid it contained—a heavy, almost colorless fluid, with none of the brilliant iridescence one would so naturally expect of such a magic compound. He shook it lovingly, almost caressingly; but there was no manifestation of its occult properties. Then he pressed open a black leather case and nodded suggestively at the hypodermic syringe on its velvet bed. The Brown-Sequard Elixir and Koch's experiments with lymph darted across my mind. I smiled with cheery doubtfulness; but he, divining my thought, made haste to say, "No, they were on the right road, but missed it."

* * * * *

He opened an inner door of the laboratory and called "Hector! Come, old fellow, come on!"

Hector was a superannuated Newfoundland who had for years been utterly worthless for anything save lying around in people's way, and in this he was an admirable success. Conceive my astonishment when a heavy, burly animal rushed in like a whirlwind and upset things generally, till finally quelled by his master. Dover looked eloquently at me, without speaking.

"But that—that isn't Hector!" I cried, doubting against doubt.

He turned up the under side of the animal's ear, and I saw two hard-lipped slits, mementoes of his wild young fighting days, when his master and I were mere lads ourselves. I remembered the wounds perfectly.

* * *

"Sixteen years old and as lively as a puppy," Dover beamed triumphantly. "I've been experimenting on him for two months. Nobody knows as yet, but won't they open their eyes when Hector runs abroad again! The plain matter of fact is I've given new lease of life with the lymph injection—same lymph as that used by earlier investigators, only they failed to clarify their compounds while I have succeeded. What is it? An animal derivative to stay and remove the effects of senility by acting upon the stagnated life-cells of any animal organism. Take the anatomical changes in Hector here, produced by infusion of the lymph compound; in the main they may be characterized as the expulsion from the bones of mineral deposits and an infiltration of the muscular tissues. Of course there are minor considerations; but these I have also overcome, not, however, without the unfortunate demise of several of my earlier animal subjects. I could not bring myself to work on Hector till failure had been eliminated from the problem. And now —"

He rose to his feet and paced excitedly up and down. It was some time before he took up his uncompleted thought.

"And now I am prepared to administer this rejuvenator to humans. And I propose, first of all, to work on one who is very dear to me—"

"Not—not—?" I quavered.

● *The Chicago-based* CONKEY'S *published two London stories in 1899 (entries 18 and 20), both containing unusual plot ideas. This one, as its title suggests, is one of London's pseudo-scientific efforts.*

Overland Monthly

Vol. XXXVII   May, 1901   No. 5

THE SCORN OF WOMAN.

BY JACK LONDON.

NCE Freda and Mrs. Eppingwell clashed. Now, Freda was a Greek girl and a dancer. At least she purported to be Greek; but this was doubted by many, for her classic face had over-much strength in it, and the tides of hell which arose in her eyes made at rare intervals her ethnology the more dubious. To a few—men—this sight had been vouchsafed, and though long years may have passed, they have not forgotten, nor will they ever forget. She never talked of herself, so that it were well to let it go down, that when in repose, expurgated, Greek she certainly was. Her furs were the most magnificent in all the country from Chilcoot to St. Michaels, and her name was common on the lips of men. But Mrs. Eppingwell was the wife of a captain; also a social constellation of the first magnitude, the path of her orbit marking the most select coterie in Dawson—a coterie captioned by the profane as the "official clique." Sitka Charley had traveled trail with her, once, when famine drew tight and a man's life was less than a cup of flour, and his judgment placed her above all women. Sitka Charley was an Indian; his criteria were primitive; but his word was flat, and his verdict a hall-mark in every camp under the circle.

These two women were man-conquering, man-subduing machines, each in her own way, and their ways were different. Mrs. Eppingwell ruled in her own house, and at the Barracks, where were younger sons galore, to say nothing of the chiefs of the police, the executive, and the judiciary. Freda ruled down in the town; but the men she ruled were the same who functioned socially at the Barracks or were fed tea and canned preserves at the hand of Mrs. Eppingwell in her hillside cabin of rough-hewn logs. Each knew the other existed; but their lives were apart as the Poles, and while they must have heard stray bits of news and were curious, they were never known to ask a question. And there would have been no trouble had not a free lance in the shape of the model-woman come into the land on the first ice, with a spanking dog-team and a cosmopolitan reputation. Loraine Lisznayi—alliterative, dramatic, and Hungarian—precipitated the strife, and because of her Mrs. Eppingwell left her hillside and invaded Freda's domain, and Freda likewise went up from the town to spread confusion and embarrassment at the Governor's ball.

All of which may be ancient history so far as the Klondike is concerned, but very few, even in Dawson, know the inner truth of the matter; nor beyond those few are there any fit to measure the wife of the captain, or the Greek dancer. And that all are now permitted to understand, let honor be accorded Sitka Charley. From his lips fell the main facts in the screed herewith presented. It ill befits that Freda herself should have waxed confidential to a mere scribbler of words, or that Mrs. Eppingwell made mention of the things which happened. They may have spoken, but it is unlikely.

II.

Floyd Vanderlip was a strong man, apparently. Hard work and hard grub had no terrors for him, as his early history in the country attested. In danger he was a lion, and when he held in check half a thousand starving men, as he once did, it was remarked that no cooler eye

● *A typical display in* Overland Monthly, *the magazine founded in 1868 and made famous by its first editor, Bret Harte. This story (entry 44) was London's ninth in* Overland *and later became the basis for a full-length London play, published as* Scorn of Women *(1906).*

TO BUILD A FIRE

BY JACK LONDON

Author of " The Call of the Wild," " The Sea-Wolf," etc.

He travels fastest who travels alone . . . but not after the frost has dropped below zero fifty degrees or more. — Yukon Code.

DAY had broken cold and gray, exceedingly cold and gray, when the man turned aside from the main Yukon trail and climbed the high earth-bank, where a dim and little-traveled trail led eastward through the fat spruce timberland. It was a steep bank, and he paused for breath at the top, excusing the act to himself by looking at his watch. It was nine o'clock. There was no sun or hint of sun, though there was not a cloud in the sky. It was a clear day, and yet there seemed an intangible pall over the face of things, a subtle gloom that made the day dark, and that was due to the absence of sun. This fact did not worry the man. He was used to the lack of sun. It had been days since he had seen the sun, and he knew that a few more days must pass before that cheerful orb, due south, would just peep above the sky-line and dip immediately from view.

The man flung a look back along the way he had come. The Yukon lay a mile wide and hidden under three feet of ice. On top of this ice were as many feet of snow. It was all pure white, rolling in gentle, snow-covered undulations where the ice-jams of the freeze-up had formed. North and south, as far as his eye could see, it was unbroken white, save for a dark hair-line that curved and twisted from around the spruce-covered island to the south, and that curved and twisted away into the north, where it disappeared behind another spruce-covered island. This dark hair-line was the trail — the main trail — that led south five hundred miles to the Chilcoot Pass, Dyea, and salt water; and that led north seventy miles to Dawson, and still on to the north a thousand miles to Nulato, and finally to St. Michael on Bering Sea, a thousand miles and half a thousand more.

But all this — the mysterious, far-reaching hair-line trail, the absence of sun from the sky, the tremendous cold, and the strangeness and weirdness of it all — made no impression on the man. It was not because he was long used to it. He was a new-comer in the land, a *chechaquo,* and this was his first winter. The trouble with him was that he was without imagination. He was quick and alert in the things of life, but only in the things, and not in the significances. Fifty degrees below zero meant eighty-odd degrees of frost. Such fact impressed him as being cold and uncomfortable, and that was all. It did not lead him to meditate upon his frailty as a creature of temperature, and upon man's frailty in general, able only to live within certain narrow limits of temperature; and from there on it did not lead him to the conjectural field of immortality and man's place in the universe. Fifty degrees below zero stood for a bite of frost that hurt and that must be guarded against by the use of mittens, ear-flaps, warm moccasins, and thick socks. Fifty degrees below zero was to him just precisely fifty degrees below zero. That there should be anything more to it than that was a thought that never entered his head.

As he turned to go on, he spat speculatively. There was a sharp, explosive crackle that startled him. He spat again. And again, in the air, before it could fall to the snow, the spittle crackled. He knew that at fifty below spittle crackled on the snow, but this spittle had crackled in the air. Undoubtedly it was colder than fifty below — how much colder he did not

● THE CENTURY MAGAZINE *paid $300 for this, the most widely read and most frequently anthologized of all Jack London short stories. Above reproduction is its original appearance (entry 108).*

Illustrated by

FRANK GODWIN

Then Bertram Cornell fought the good fight, the first for a good cause in all his life, and the last. The bone-barbed missiles flew about him like hail.

A Northland Miracle

By JACK LONDON

THIS is a story of things that happened, which goes to show that there is an eternal core of goodness in the hearts of all men. Bertram Cornell was a bad man, and a failure. In a little English home overseas there had been sorrow unavailing and tears shed in vain for his earthly and spiritual welfare. He was bad, utterly bad. There could be no doubt of it. Thoughtless, careless and uncaring were mild terms with which to brand his weaknesses.

Even in his boyhood he had been strong only for evil. Kind words and pleadings had had no effect on him, and he had been callous to the wet eyes of his mother and sisters and the sterner though no less kindly admonitions of his father. So it could hardly have been otherwise, when yet a very young man, that he fled hurriedly out of his home in England, carrying with him something which should have burdened his conscience had he but possessed one, and leaving behind a disgrace on his name for his people to bear. And so it was that those who had known him spoke of him in bitterness and sadness, until the memory of him was dimmed with time. Of what further evils he wrought there was never a whisper, and of his end no one ever heard. In his last hour he made recompense and wiped clean his tarnished page of life. But he did this thing in a far country, where news travels slowly and gets lost upon the way, and where men ofttimes die before they

can tell how others died. But this was the way of it. Strong of body and uncaring, he had laughed at the great rough hand of the world and had always done, not what the world demanded, but whatever Bertram Cornell desired. And he had met harsh words with harsher, and stout blows with stouter. He had served as sailor on many seas, as sheepherder on the Australian ranges, as cowboy among the Dakota cattlemen, and as an enrolled private with the Mounted Police of the Northwest Territory. From this last post he had deserted on the discovery of gold in the Klondike and worked his way to the Alaskan coast. Here, because of his frontier experience, he speedily found place to fit into in a party of three other men.

This party was bound for the Klondike, but it had planned to abandon the beaten track and to go into .he country over a new and untraveled route. With a pack train of many horses (cayuses from the mountains of eastern Oregon), the four men struck east into the desolate wilderness which lies be-

yond Mount St. Elias, and then north through the upland region in which the headwaters of the White and Tanana rivers have their source. It was an unexplored domain, marked vaguely on the maps, which was yet to feel the foot of the first white man. So vast and dismal was it that even animal life was scarce, and the tiny Indian tribes few and far between. For days, sometimes, they rode through the silent forest or by the rims of lonely lakes and saw no living thing, and the sobbing of the waters. A great solemnity brooded over the land, and the quiet was so profound that they came to hush their voices and to waste few words in idle talk.

AS they journeyed on they prospected for the hidden gold, groping in the chill pools of the torrents and panning dirt in the shadows of the mighty glaciers. Once they came upon a body of virgin copper, like a mountain, but they could only shrug their shoulders and pass on. Food for their horses

was scarce, and quite often poisonous, and the patient animals died one by one on the strange trail their masters had led them to. Crossing a high divide, the party was overwhelmed by a sleety storm common to such elevations, and, when finally they struggled through to the warmer valley beneath, the last horse had been left behind.

But here, in the sheltered valley, John Thornton cleared back the moss and from the grass-roots shook out glittering particles of yellow gold. Bertram Cornell was with him at the time, and that night the twain carried back to camp nuggets which weighed a thousand dollars in the scales. A stop was called, and, at the end of a month the four men had mined a treasure far greater than they could carry. But their food supply had been steadily growing less and less, till one man could bend forward and bear it all on his back.

What with the bleak region and fall coming on, it was high time to be going along. Somewhere to the northeast they knew the Klondike lay and the country of the Yukon. How far they did not know, though they thought it could not be more than a hundred miles. So each took about five pounds of gold, or a thousand dollars, and the rest of the great treasure they cached safely against their return. And to return they intended just as soon as they could lay in more grub. Their ammunition having

THE Semi-MONTHLY
MAGAZINE SECTION
APPEARING THE FIRST AND THIRD SUNDAYS OF EACH MONTH
THE *San Francisco* CALL

San Francisco, Cal., Sunday, December 1, 1912

E.P.Upjohn

Jack London
in This Issue

"The Captain of The Susan Drew"

A Magazine for Your Reading Table

Having secured the entire Short Story Output of Jack London for 1913 The Semi-Monthly Magazine Section will publish one each month.

● *Despite the boast printed at the bottom of this cover page, London published only one short story in 1913 and that appeared in* The Bookman. *This tale (entry 172) was resurrected in 1931 and was republished with a few revisions in* Physical Culture *magazine.*

Dear Mrs. Lane —

Wishing you a merry Christmas, & with many remembrances of your kind friendship,

Jack London

Christmas, 1904.

● *This sample of London's handwriting is a book inscription—possibly from the first edition of* THE SEA WOLF, *published in October, 1904. (Dale L. Walker Collection)*

● *Four views of Jack London. Upper left, a photo made in 1914 as he was en route to Mexico for his last stint as a war correspondent. Upper right, a photo published in connection with a review of* THE SON OF THE WOLF, *his first book. Lower left, a cartoon by James Montgomery Flagg (1877-1960) whose famous Uncle Sam "I Want You" poster was used to recruit during World War I. Lower right, a photograph made by Tesio of Oakland, California.*

ACKNOWLEDGEMENTS

THIS WORK would have been impossibly incomplete without the research and editing abilities of Mr. James E. Sisson III of Berkeley, California. Mr. Sisson, without question the best-grounded of all Jack London scholars, has devoted many years to London research, a major part of which has been the uncovering of the most obscure of the author's published writings — and many of these are obscure indeed — as well as many unpublished pieces such as London's plays, several of which are cited in the annotations in this work.

Special gratitude is extended to Dr. Hensley Woodbridge and Dr. Franklin Walker, quoted in the Introduction, and to Mr. Tony Bubka of Berkeley; Mr. George Tweney of Seattle, Washington; Mr. Jerry Stewart of Wayne, N. J.; Mr. Russ Kingman of Oakland, California; Mr. Richard Weiderman of Cedar Springs, Michigan; and Prof. Vil M. Bykov of the Academy of Sciences of the U.S.S.R., Moscow. All have, through their correspondence and without knowing it, contributed to this work. None, of course, are responsible for any errors or interpretations within.

Two of Jack London's biographers were of inestimable help in various ways: the late Joan London, to whom the work is dedicated, and Mr. Richard O'Connor of Ellsworth, Maine.

In addition, I am greatly indebted to Mrs. Jeanne Reynolds and Mrs. Yvonne Greear of the U.T. El Paso Library for countless — and usually eleventh-hour — chores of rounding up obscure bits of information from obscure periodicals; to the reference department of the El Paso Public Library; to Prof. Haldeen Braddy of the Department of English at the University, and Dean Ray Small of the School of Liberal Arts at U.T. El Paso, for their examination of the manuscript and always helpful suggestions; and to Dr. Evan Haywood Antone, Editor of the Texas Western Press, and Dr. Carl Hertzog, Director of the Press, for their sustained interest in the project.

INDEX

(All numerals refer to *entries* in the Fiction Chronology)